Gasparo Contarini

THE OFFICE OF A BISHOP

(*De Officio viri boni et probi episcopi*)

Introduced, Translated and Edited
by
John Patrick Donnelly, S.J.

MARQUETTE
UNIVERSITY

PRESS

Milwaukee, 2002

REFORMATION TEXTS WITH TRANSLATION
(1350-1650)
Kenneth Hagen, General Editor.
Series: Theology and Piety, Volume 1
Ian Levy, Editor

Cover design by Sean Donnelly
based on an engraving of Gasparo Contarini
in the Museo Civico Correr, Venice

Layout and production: Joan Skocir

Library of Congress Cataloging-in-Publication Data

Contarini, Gasparo, 1483-1542
 [De officio viri boni et probi episcopi. English & Latin]
 The office of a bishop = De officio viri boni et probi episcopi /
Gasparo Contarini ; introduced, translated, and edited by John Patrick
Donnelly.
  p. cm. — (Reformation texts with translation (1350-1650).
Theology and piety ; v. 1)
  English and Latin.
  Includes bibliographical references and index.
  ISBN 0-87462-706-0 (pbk. : alk. paper)
  1. Catholic Church—Bishops. I. Donnelly, John Patrick, 1934-
II. Title. III. Series.
BX1905 .C6613 2002
262'.122—dc21

                                            2002001434

Member, THE ASSOCIATION OF AMERICAN UNIVERSITY PRESSES

MARQUETTE UNIVERSITY PRESS
MILWAUKEE

The Association of Jesuit University Presses
2002

This book is dedicated to John R. Sheets: Jesuit,

priest, teacher, theologian, Auxiliary Bishop

emeritus of Fort Wayne-South Bend

CONTENTS

Preface...5

Introduction...7

Bibliography...23

TEXTS

  Book One

    Latin text...26

    English text...27

  Book Two

    Latin text...72

    English text...73

  Appendix

    Latin text...128

    English text...129

Index...134

PREFACE

I began this project in 1993. In the summer of 1995 I spent a week going over manuscripts of Contarini's *De officio episcopi* at the Vatican Library, but on returning to Marquette University I had to turn my attention to two other books I was editing. Over the last eight years I have incurred many debts. Most important was the encouragement and advice of the two leading Contarini scholars, Gigliola Fragnito and Elisabeth Gleason. Professor Gleason made suggestions which improved the Introduction, and I have also drawn heavily on both their published works. I am grateful for the help of two research assistants: Timothy McDonnell did most of the work of transcribing the Latin text of 1571 to my computer while Joseph Persivale adapted the text to new software. Martin O'Keefe, S.J., of the Institute of Jesuit Sources at St. Louis University checked my translation for errors. Three Jesuits in my community at Marquette University provided assistance: William Dooley helped me with references to Aristotle and Plato, Roland Teske gave sage advice about translating a number of difficult passages, and James Grummer caught slips in the Introduction. Drs. Ian Levy and Kenneth Hagen of Marquette's Theology Department suggested corrections in the translation and additions in the Introduction. I also owe thanks to the librarians at both the Biblioteca Vaticana and Marquette University for their help. I remain responsible for any errors.

John Patrick Donnelly, S.J.
Marquette University
January 29, 2001

INTRODUCTION

GASPARO CONTARINI (1483-1542)

Gasparo Contarini was born 16 October 1483 at Venice. His life breaks down into four periods: his education up to 1509; his years as a free-lance scholar, 1509 to 1518; his service to the Venetian state, 1518-1535; and his career as churchman, 1535-1542.[1]

EDUCATION

The Contarini were among Venice's most distinguished families. Eight Contarini served Venice as doges between 1043 and 1688.[2] Gasparo was the eldest son of Alvise di Federico dei Contarini and had seven brothers and five sisters. Their family's wealth derived from trading, especially in Egypt and in Apulia along Italy's Adriatic coast, but like many aristocratic Venetian families, as Venetian trade declined in the eastern Mediterranean, the Contarini diversified by buying land in the Veneto, especially near Padua. Gasparo's early education was under a family tutor at Venice; in 1501 he entered the University of Padua, arguably the world's best university after Paris and continued his studies there until 1509. Like many aristocrats, he did not take a degree, but he was a keen and dedicated student whose interests ranged over Latin and Greek literature, medicine, mathematics, astronomy, and especially theology and philosophy; soon after leaving Padua he wrote treatises in several different disciplines. His best-known teacher at Padua was Pietro Pomponazzi, Europe's leading expert on Aristotle.[3] So dedicated was Contarini to intellectual pursuits that when his father died in 1502, he entrusted the

---

[1] The best guide to Contarini's life as well as an introduction to his writings is Elisabeth Gleason, *Gasparo Contarini: Venice, Rome and Reform* (Berkeley: University of California Press, 1993).

[2] The *Dizionario biografico degli italiani* (Rome: Istituto della Enciclopedia italiana, 1960-) [henceforward DBI] vol. 28, pp. 70-330, has articles on more than seventy Venetian Contarini. That on Gasparo Contarini by Gigliola Fragnito, 72-92, is easily the longest.

[3] On the University of Padua, see *Encyclopedia of the Renaissance* (New York: Scribner's, 1999) IV, 358-362. On Pomponazzi, Ibid., V, 116-118.

family business interests to his younger brothers. He left the University in 1509 only because Padua was under siege.

THE FREE-LANCE SCHOLAR, 1509-1518

While at Padua Contarini developed friendships with other Venetian patricians. Two close friends, Tommaso Giustiniani and Vincenzo Querini, were deeply religious, as was Contarini. Giustiniani decided to become a Camaldolese monk in 1510 and was joined by Querini the next year. The three kept up an extensive correspondence in which the two Camaldolese urged Contarini to leave the world and join them. This led to a spiritual crisis for Contarini which climaxed on Holy Saturday 1511 and resulted in two convictions. First that he could and should serve God in the world rather than in a monastery, and second that Christians cannot attain salvation through their own efforts and good works but only by being justified through the righteousness of Christ. Several scholars have seen this intense spiritual experience of 1511 as parallel to Martin Luther's famous tower experience of justification by faith alone. Certainly it conditioned Contarini's theology of grace and disposed him to be sympathetic to this aspect of Luther's teaching. In 1515 Contarini recovered from a period of ill health and visited Florence where he became friends with several leading Florentine intellectuals and engaged in conversation about the political institutions of ancient Greece and Rome which later contributed to his best-known book, *De magistratibus et Republica Venetorum*. In 1516 Pomponazzi published at Bologna his *De immortalitate animae* which argued that the soul's immortality could not be proven by human reason and was not taught by Aristotle. He sent Contarini a copy and asked for his reaction to it. Contarini replied with his own *De immortalitate animae*, which was written in the summer of 1517, during the same months he was writing his book on the duty of a bishop. He asserted that reason can prove the immortality of the soul. This was topic of considerable interest at the time because the Fifth Lateran Council had condemned in 1513 unnamed Averroists and Aristotelians for claiming that the human soul was mortal or that all people shared the same soul. Contarini's tract was in two books; the first was published anonymously at Bologna in 1518 together with a reply by Pomponazzi; the second book appeared only in his *Opera* published by Gasparo's nephew Alvise Contarini in 1571.

THE VENETIAN MAGISTRATE, 1518-1535

In 1518 Contarini began his service to the Venetian state which constituted the longest part of his adult life. The prestige of his family and the circle of friends he had established among the Venetian elite made his climb to increasingly important posts fairly easy. His first post was quite minor, supervising irrigation projects and land sales in the Po delta with a view to reducing state debt. Late in 1520 he was entrusted with a major post, ambassador to Emperor Charles V. He joined the Emperor at the famous Diet of Worms of 1521 which condemned Martin Luther. The Venetian government was less interested in theological controversy in Germany than in the chronic friction between Charles V and Francis I of France; since Venice leaned toward France, Contarini's role at the Imperial court was difficult, but he managed to win the personal esteem of the Emperor. Few great rulers in history moved about as much as Charles V; Contarini followed him from Germany to the Netherlands, England and finally Spain where Contarini stayed writing detailed reports to the Venetian Senate from 1522 to 1525. The cost of serving as ambassador far outstripped his pay; even though helped financially by his brothers, Contarini was forced to resign and take a minor post in supervising the administration of Venice's mainland possessions along with serving as the military governor of Brescia. In 1528 the Senate elected Contarini ambassador to Pope Clement VII; Contarini's task at Rome was complicated because the Venetian government taxed the clergy heavily, controlled church appointments and had occupied two cities, Cervia and Ravenna, which had been under papal control. For Venetians even more depressing was Venice's decline from great power status, the repeated wars of Charles V and Francis I, and the rising power of the Turks on land and sea.

In 1530 Contarini returned to Venice to serve on a key advisory committee of six men; later the same year he was elected to the famous Council of Ten which supervised security in the Venetian state. There followed several other appointments to major posts, several held concurrently. For instance, he was one of three officials who supervised the University of Padua and was an advisor to the doge.

During his years in office, especially when he was ambassador in Spain and had time on his hands, he continued to write treatises. The most important was *De magistratibus et Republica Venetorum*,

which not only described Venice's political institutions and structure but argued that these were the secret to the Most Serene Republic's stability and dedication to republican ideals in an age when despots had replaced republican governments in most Italian city states. The work was published in 1543, with translations into Italian and French (1544) and later into English (1599). While in Spain he wrote his *Primae philosophiae compendium.* He also wrote a tract on logic and a long tract in five books on Aristotelian cosmology. More interesting for his later career as churchman were his attack on the Augsburg Confession (*Confutatio articulorum seu questionum lutheranorum*) and a brief defense of papal power (*De potestate pontificis quod divinitus sit tradita*). In 1536 he wrote a letter/tract to the famous poet Vittoria Colonna on free will.

CONTARINI AS CHURCHMAN, 1535-1542

In October 1534 Paul III was elected pope; he has considerable claim to be the first reform pope. The next May he named Contarini a cardinal, to the delight of Venice. Paul III may have been motivated by Contarini's reputation as a scholar, his political experience and the favor which he enjoyed with Charles V. Contarini quickly took orders as a priest and bishop at a time when many cardinals did not receive sacred orders. In 1536 he was named bishop of Belluno, although his administrative duties for the pope prevented him from visiting his diocese—this in contrast to how he insisted that bishops live and work in their dioceses in the *The Office of a Bishop.* Contarini did not follow the example of many cardinals in seeking lucrative benefices.

Contarini chaired the commission which drew up the famous Counsel on Reforming the Church of 1537. Few of its sweeping recommendations were implemented by Paul III, largely because they would have undermined papal finances. Contarini was among the leaders of reform-minded churchmen such as Cardinals Reginald Pole and Giovanni Morone called the *spirituali*; they embraced a doctrine of justification with affinities to Luther's teaching, even though they opposed his teaching on sacraments and church order.[4] Contarini was also a strong supporter of the new Jesuit order.

[4] The literature on the *spirituali* and their theological views is very large. Good starting points are the following: Elisabeth G. Gleason, "On the Nature of Sixteenth Century Italian Evangelism: Scholarship, 1953-1978," *Sixteenth Century*

The pinnacle of Contarini's career came in 1541 when he was appointed papal legate to the Colloquy at Regensburg called by Charles V to see if theological differences between Catholics and Lutherans could be ironed out. The main Protestant representatives were Philipp Melanchthon and Martin Bucer, while the official Catholic theologians were Johann Eck, Johannes Gropper and Julius Pflug. John Calvin was there but without official status. Luther could not attend because he was technically an outlaw. Initially the colloquy scored what seemed a breakthrough, a statement on justification partly crafted by Contarini which both sides accepted; but discussions reached an impasse on the sacraments, and thorny questions about church structures and the papacy were never taken up. The colloquy broke up on 22 May 1541. Contarini wrote a treatise defending the Regensburg formula on justification, but neither Luther nor Rome found it acceptable. In the aftermath of Regensburg Paul III set up the Roman Inquisition and put the militant Cardinal Gianpietro Carafa (later Paul IV) in charge of it. Some *spirituali*, notably Bernardino Ochino and Peter Martyr Vermigli, fled to Geneva or Zurich.[5] Contarini's stock at Rome seemed in decline. On his return to Italy Paul III named him legate/governor at Bologna, the second largest city in the papal states, suggesting that he still enjoyed the Pope's esteem, but he was now removed from the mainstream of policy. Just before his death, at the request of his friend Cardinal Giovanni Morone, he wrote a short catechism upholding the traditional Catholic faith.[6] He died at Bologna 24 August 1542.

Journal 9 (1978) 3-25; Anne J. Schutte, "Periodization of Sixteenth-Century Italian Religious History: The Post-Cantimori Paradigm Shift," *Journal of Modern History* 61 (1989) 260-284; Dermot Fenlon, *Heresy and Obedience in Tridentine Italy. Cardinal Pole and the Counter Reformation* (Cambridge: Cambridge University Press, 1972); Thomas Mayer, *Reginald Pole: Prince and Prophet* (Cambridge: Cambridge University Press, 2000). For Contarini's relations with the *spirituali*, see Gleason's biography of Contarini, 191-197, 260-276, 290-299.

[5] Gigliola Fragnito, "Gli 'Spirituali' e la fuga di Bernardino Ochino," *Rivista storica italiana* 84 (1972) 777-813. Philip McNair, *Peter Martyr in Italy: An Anatomy of Apostasy* (Oxford: Clarendon Press, 1967) 239-293.

[6] On Contarini's catechism see Franz Josef Kötter, *Die Eucharistielehre in den katholischen Katechismen des 16. Jahrhunderts bis zum Erscheinen des Catechismus romanus (1566)* (Münster, 1969.) 84-85, 235-238.

CONTARINI'S *DE OFFICIO EPISCOPI*

THE LITERATURE ON THE OFFICE OF A BISHOP

The original full title of Contarini's tract was *De officio viri boni et probi episcopi* (On the office [or duty] of a good man and upright bishop), but it is usually referred to by a short title: *De officio episcopi*, which we have translated as *The Office of a Bishop*. The Renaissance was awash with books on how to perform certain roles in society. Two of the most famous were written in Italy within a few years of Contarini's treatise, Niccolò Machiavelli's *The Prince* (written in 1513) and Baldassar Castiglione's *The Book of the Courtier* (written between 1515 and 1519); like Contarini's treatise both circulated some years in manuscript before publication. Giovanni Della Casa, Contarini's friend and biographer, wrote *Galateo*, which rivalled Castiglione's work as guide to a gentleman's behavior. Most such books were written to guide kings and rulers, but there was no lack of books instructing bishops on how to fulfill their duties. Some of them went back to the patristic age. Thus St. John Chrysostom wrote a treatise on the priesthood.[7] The most important patristic treatises on the duties of the clergy were St. Gregory the Great's *Liber regulae pastoralis*[8] (591) and St. Ambrose's *De officiis ministrorum*, written about 391; this last may have been the only one of all such treatises that Contarini borrowed from.[9] He cites none of them explicitly. He seems equally unaware of the medieval treatises such as the *De officiis episcoporum* by Hincmar, Archbishop of Rheims.[10] The Renaissance and Reformation periods produced many similar treatises. St. Lorenzo Giustiniani (1381-1456), bishop of Venice, wrote *De Institutione et regimini praelatorum*, but its call for mystical union with God strikes a very different note than does Contarini.[11] Claude Jay, one of Ignatius of Loyola's earliest companions, wrote *Speculum praesulis* as a gift for Cardinal Truchsess. Two books on the duties of cardinals were Paolo Cortese's *De Cardinalatu* (1510) and Giovanni Botero's *Ufficio del*

---

[7] *Patrologia Graeca*, 48, 623-692.

[8] *Patrologia Latina*, 77, 13-128.

[9] *Patrologia Latina*, 16, 25-184.

[10] *Patrologia Latina* 125, 1087-1094.

[11] His *Opera* were published in Brescia in 1506; there were several later editions. On his treatise see Oliver Logan, "The Ideal of the Bishop and the Venetian Patriciate: c. 1430-c. 1630," *Journal of Ecclesiastical History* 29 (1978) 419-423.

Cardinale (1599). The works of Tellechea Idigoras and Piton in the bibliography at the end of this Introduction examine Spanish and French treatises on the duties of bishops.

Sixteenth-century Italy produced several model bishops, the most famous being Gian Matteo Giberti, St. Carlo Borromeo, and Gabriele Paleotti; all have been studied recently. Less well known is Agostino Valier, who came closer in spirit to Contarini than the other three, partly because like Contarini he illustrated a gentler approach to correcting abuses and less personal austerity than Borromeo, and he took more care in avoiding friction with government authorities. In this he and Contarini were distinctively Venetian. Valier wrote three treatises on the office of high churchmen which were published several times in the sixteenth century: *Episcopus, Cardinalis* and *Vita Caroli Borromei. Episcopus,* the first and most important, was written at the request of Carlo Borromeo. Perhaps even more interesting is Valier's letter to Federico Borromeo, "De cauta imitatione sanctorum episcoporum," which cautioned Federico to moderate his uncle's personal austerity, harshness in imposing discipline, and inflexibility toward civil officials. Contarini would have agreed. Valier highlights a key factor in Borromean and Tridentine reform which Contarini never touches on: diocesan synods.[12]

THE COMPOSITION OF CONTARINI'S TREATISE

Two things are most striking about Contarini's treatise on the duty of a bishop. First, it was written in 1517, a few months before Martin Luther posted his Ninety-five Theses and changed the history of Christianity. Luther and Contarini were born a few months apart; Contarini died four years before Luther. Their pivotal "tower experiences" may have been about the same time, although Luther's is hard to date exactly. Secondly, Contarini was still a layman. Almost all previous treatises on the duties of bishops were written by bishops who had considerable experience in pastoral care. Thus Contarini helps us see what a learned and devout layman expected of the hierarchy on the eve of the Reformation. Surely many others shared his expectations. Ironically, Pietro Lippomano who had requested the treatise from Contarini represents much of what was

[12] Ibid., 433-441. Logan goes on to review several other Venetian treatises, 441-449. For his treatment of Contarini's treatise, 423-434.

worst in the bishops of their day. He was still a teenager when elected
bishop of Bergamo, even though canon law set the minimum age for
bishops at thirty. Lippomano served as bishop elect until his episcopal consecration in 1530, when he could finally carry out all the
sacramental duties of a bishop. He was named as successor of his
uncle Nicolao Lippomano, who planned to keep most of the income
from the bishopric in his own hands, but death overtook him a month
after he renounced his bishopric in favor of his nephew. Clearly this
was a case of nepotism, but the Venetian patriciate, which controlled
church appointments throughout Venetian territory, was willing to
ignore canon law in favor of leading Venetian families. A papal
consistory ratified Pietro's appointment.[13] Contarini alludes discreetly
to Lippomano's youth in the letter he sent Lippomano with the treatise and mentions Pietro's training in classical letters and canon law,
but this must have been meager, and he would have known little if
any theology. A cynic might dismiss the treatise as an example of the
blind leading the blind. But certainly Lippomano needed advice des-
perately, and as readers will see, much of the advice was wise. We do
not know why young Lippomano asked Contarini for advice; probably they had met and may have discussed the forthcoming appointment of Lippomano, who almost certainly looked up to Contarini
and respected his judgment.

THE STRUCTURE OF CONTARINI'S TREATISE

Contarini's treatise, written in the summer of 1517 when
Contarini was thirty-three, is the work of a scholar whose recent studies, as he points out in his introductory letter to Pietro Lippomano,
had been devoted largely to the study of philosophy, especially Aristotle
and Thomas Aquinas. The work is divided into two books.
The first book is shorter, more abstract and less interesting.[14] It
begins with an introduction which examines how human beings are
images of God, how they compare with angels, and why as social
beings they need leaders. This leads to short discussions comparing

---

[13] Gleason, *Gasparo Contarini*, 93; Fragnito, *Gasparo Contarini*, 80-82.

[14] "Altogether, the first book of the *De officio episcopi* is academic in the worst
sense, unoriginal and uninspiring. It was most surely the concrete programme of
action enunciated in the second book that gave the treatise its reputation." Oliver
Logan, 429.

bishops to kings and explaining episcopal dignity. Contarini then explores the virtues and their relationship to human nature. He divides human virtues into three groups. First are those virtues related to the irascible and concupiscible parts of the soul: temperance, liberality, fortitude, magnanimity, magnificence and gentleness. Next come two virtues related to the rational soul, justice and prudence, plus a short reflection of Christian perfection. Finally Contarini examines the three theological virtues of faith, hope and charity. He then tries to relate the discussion of the virtues to the knowledge a good bishop should possess and how he should put helping his people above his own convenience—here Contarini condemns the absenteeism so common among bishops of his day. Book I draws heavily on Contarini's study of Aristotle's and Aquinas's treatment of the soul and the virtues. It is worth observing that Book I refers only seven times to the Bible; this part of his tract owes much more to Aristotle and Thomas Aquinas.[15]

Book II is longer, more complex, practical, religious and interesting. It begins by arguing that human beings need divine revelation, the sacraments and the clergy. Contarini then gives a sort of daily schedule for the good bishop, much of it structured around the Divine Office which priests and bishops were obliged to pray every day, although he includes mental prayer, Bible reading and Mass in the daily schedule. The bulk of the bishop's morning should be devoted to conferring with his flock and priests. The afternoon is more leisurely and allows time for recreation, conversing with friends, and listening to music. The bishop should allow flexibility in his schedule and should feel free to make excursions into the countryside for recreation and spiritual reflection.

The longest part of the treatise deals with the actual duties of the bishop toward differing groups within his flock. His discussion takes up first men, then women. Crucial are the clergy of the diocese. Contarini discusses how the bishop should deal with bad priests and the care he should devote to ordaining good priests and supervising their education. He then discusses country priests and members of

---

[15] Oliver Logan, *The Venetian Upper Clergy in the 16th and 17th Centuries: A Study in Religious Culture* (Lewiston: Edwin Mellen Press, 1996) also stresses the influence of Aquinas (170-176) and the relatively small role of scripture (175): "In the bulk of Contarini's religious writing, Scriptural exposition is conspicuous by its absense."

religious orders. The bishop's main task is preaching; he must stand up for the faith by opposing impiety, heresy, superstition and abuses. The faith must be God-centered, but allows for a proper cult of the saints. Sinners must be admonished and youth must be properly trained. Contarini is more succinct in his recommendations about a bishop's dealing with women because, except for nuns, their fathers and husbands have a more direct care over them; but he does make some recommendations about attire, widows and orphans.

He devotes separate consideration to sharing episcopal wealth, dealing with obligations of justice and charity, personal frugality, and the claims different groups have of the church's charity. Hospitals and peasants are treated. A short conclusion follows.[16] Three times Contarini points to Pietro Barozzi, the bishop of Padua when Contarini was a student there, and he holds up for imitation Barozzi's devotion to preaching, a task most Renaissance bishops avoided.[17]

In the cover letter which Contarini sent with his text to Pietro Lippomano he tells Lippomano that he had originally planned to add a third book which would illustrate the points made in Books I and II by concrete historical examples, but that would have involved Contarini in considerable research which his other duties did not permit.

Contarini's treatise as a whole suggests a life style for a bishop which did not differ too much from that of a devout country gentleman who had to look after his estates, servants and peasants—a far cry from the hectic pace of a Carlo Borromeo. Contarini, here very much the Venetian aristocrat, urges young Lippomano to avoid friction with the civil government, almost to the point of subservience—again very different from Borromeo's confrontations with the Spanish viceroy at Milan.[18]

---

[16] Fragnito gives a detailed discussion of the contents of Contarini's treatise in her *Gasparo Contarini*, 152-206. Silvio Tramontin also summarizes the contents in his "Il 'De officio episcopi' di Gasparo Contarini" *Studia Patavina* 12 (1965) 292-302. Other summaries are found in Oliver Logan, *The Venetian Upper Clergy*, 159-167, and in Hubert Jedin and Giuseppe Alberigo, *Il Tipo ideale di vescovo secondo la riforma cattolica* (Brescia: Morcelliana, 1985) 25-29.

[17] Jedin, Ibid., 28-29. Logan devotes a chapter to Barozzi, 107-145. Also DBI 4, 510-512.

[18] Shortly before his death Borromeo wrote a long letter to Bishop Andrea Bathory describing the life style of a good bishop. To cite only one sentence, he advises Bathory that he will never attain chaste living "unless you afflict your flesh by fasting, repress all your senses, flee leisure like a plague, and avoid all familiarity not just with women but also with all whose lives do not shine with the splendor of chastity." The letter is printed in the *Monumenta Poloniae Vaticana* (Krakow: Polska Akademia Umiejetnosci, 1950) VII, 685-688.

THIS TEXT AND TRANSLATION

This text and translation share with those of Savonarola and Melanchthon that I have done for this series the goal of making available a text and a translation with modern notes and introduction. Having text and translation on facing pages should help those not familiar with Renaissance Latin, especially graduate students, to improve their skill at reading post-classical Latin. This text, however, tries to do something more. The Latin texts of Savonarola and Melanchthon are available in good modern editions. Contarini's text in available only in the three sixteenth-century editions of his *Opera*, and the whole text has never been translated into English.[19] Texts published by their authors during their lifetime usually present few difficulties for editors. Contarini's text was not published until twenty-nine years after his death, and variant readings present a considerable challenge to an editor. But they also present an opportunity because the main variant readings are not due to stylistic modifications but to the censorship of Counter Reformation Catholicism. These variations then offer an excellent opportunity to observe such censorship in detail. There are three main versions of the text: manuscript readings, the 1571 Paris edition (the first printed edition), and the two (identical) Venetian editions of 1578 and 1589. The manuscripts clearly come closest to what Contarini himself wrote. The printed versions differ from one another and even more from the manuscript versions because of Counter Reformation censorship.

Here background on how and why Contarini's writings came to be printed is useful. The subject has been investigated in detail by Gigliola Fragnito, and our account tries to summarize her research.[20] During Contarini's lifetime only a portion of one work, his *De immortalitate animae,* was printed although manuscripts of his writings circulated. After his death his family wanted to enhance his reputation and theirs by having his works published, and several works

---

[19] There is a partial translation, mostly from Book II in John Olin, editor, *The Catholic Reformation: Savonarola to Ignatius Loyola* (New York: Harper and Row, 1969) 90-106.

[20] Fragnito first published her research on this subject in "Aspetti della censura ecclesiastica nell' Europa della Controriforma: l'edizione parigina delle opere di Gasparo Contarini," *Rivista di storia e letteratura religiosa* 21 (1985) 3-48. I have used the reprint of her article in her *Gasparo Contarini: un magistrato veneziano al servizio della cristianità* (Florence: Olschki, 1988) 307-368.

began appearing in print, starting with his *De magistratibus et Republica Venetorum* in 1543. Publishing his theological writings presented a greater problem because the Protestant Reformation north of the Alps, the flight of Ochino, Vermigli and others in 1542, and the emergence of scattered Protestant communities in Italy, especially at Lucca and Modena, sent shock waves through Italy and led to the establishment of the Roman Inquisition in 1542 under the militant Cardinal Gianpietro Carafa. Carafa later became Pope Paul IV, and his pontificate from 1555 to 1559 marked the most repressive phase of the Counter Reformation. Carafa had long been suspicious of the *spirituali*. During his pontificate Cardinal Giovanni Morone was arrested and investigated by the Inquisition, and Cardinal Reginald Pole also came under suspicion. Pole had fallen one vote short of being elected pope in 1549. Both had been friends of Contarini. Pius IV (1559-1565) rehabilitated Morone and charged him with reassembling the Council of Trent. But the election of Pius V (1565-1572) brought renewed militancy. These developments at Rome meant that Alvise Contarini, Gasparo's nephew who was the main driving force for the publication of Gasparo's works, needed to move with caution.[21] He was encouraged in this by Cardinal Morone. He enlisted several scholars to help toward the publications of Gasparo's works, although the precise contribution of these scholars in adapting Contarini's works to the new defensive mentality of the Counter Reformation is not fully clear.

Merely gathering Contarini's manuscripts presented problems since they were scattered in collections at Venice, Rome and Bologna. Two treatises that he had loaned to friends were never recovered. Some of his works were published without authorization from his relatives. The roles of Contarini's relatives and his secretary, friend and later biographer Ludovico Beccadelli in trying to gather these materials also remain unclear.[22]

---

[21] On Alvise Contarini (1537-1579) see the article by G. Cozzi in DBI 28, 78-81. Fragnito (*Gasparo Contarini*, 308) observes that the history of the Paris edition of Contarini's works was closely tied to the history of the *spirituali*; it was also linked to their opponents in the Italian hierarchy. She also notes that Alvise Contarini belonged to the "vecchi," the faction of the Venetian aristocracy which fostered good relations with Rome, partly for theological reasons but partly because they saw in heresy a threat to Venice's political and social serenity. Ibid.

[22] Ibid., 308-311, 319. On Beccadelli, see DBI 7, 407-413.

In publishing his works Contarini's friends and relatives were trying to protect his reputation from secret investigations being carried on by the Inquisition at Rome and to refute rumors questioning his orthodoxy. Thus four of his short theological works were published at Florence in 1553, probably by his *spirituali* friends, although this is uncertain.[23] The Contarini family commissioned another friend, the esteemed author Giovanni Della Casa, to write Gasparo's biography in 1553, but he died in 1556 without having completed it, so the task was passed on to Pietro Vettori. This biography, which has been called the life of a wise pagan more than a holy bishop, was printed as an introduction to the various editions of Contarini's *Opera*.[24] When Gianpietro Carafa was elected pope in 1555, the Contarini family and their friends seem to have postponed plans for publishing Gasparo's writings till a better time, but they recruited Egidio Foscarari, O.P., and Paolo Manuzio to work on the project.[25] Ludovico Beccadelli, who had served as Contarini's secretary, was encouraged to write a second biography; written in Italian and later translated into Latin, it is a more satisfactory historical source than the Della Casa-Vettori biography. In turn Beccadelli encouraged Alvise Contarini in 1561 (after the death of Paul IV) to sponsor a fine edition of Gasparo's works.[26] Early in 1562 the Council of Trent was again in session, and there seem to have been meetings at Trent which included Morone, Giulio Contarini (Gasparo's nephew and bishop of Belluno),[27] Alvise Contarini, Matteo Dandolo (Gasparo's brother-in-law)[28] and Beccadelli which discussed plans to publish a complete edition of Contarini's works.[29] Alvise Contarini wrote to Foscarari, bishop of Modena, on 14 November 1563 that "we can securely resolve to have printed that part which seems good to a prudent judgment."[30] The task of making revisions seems to have been entrusted to Foscarari in 1563 at the urging of Cardinal Morone, but Foscarari probably had not finished the task before his death the next year. It is

---

[23] Ibid., 316-318.

[24] Ibid., 320-321, 331, 342. For Della Casa, DBI 36, 699-719.

[25] Ibid., 326. On Foscarari, who had been responsible for editing many of Reginald Pole's writings, see DBI 49, 280-282.

[26] Fragnito, *Gasparo Contarini*, 321, 330-331, 341.

[27] DBI 28, 218-224.

[28] DBI 32, 492-495.

[29] Fragnito, *Gasparo Contarini*, 341.

[30] Ibid., 343.

not known who completed the preparation of the manuscript, which was submitted to the Faculty of Theology at Paris in 1570 for approval. That manuscript has never been located.[31]

The massive volume in folio appeared late in 1571. At the end of the table of contents is printed the approval of the Theology Faculty dated the Kalends of December 1570. It states that "nobody could find in [this volume] something which is inconsistent with the Catholic Church or the very holy sanctions of the Fathers or which could offend any devout person and Christian reader." The good doctors of the Sorbonne could not have been more wrong. On 16 February 1572 Cardinal Scipione Rebiba, the commissary of the Inquisition, forbade the sale of the book until it had been diligently revised. A public notice to this effect was sent to booksellers on 22 March 1574.[32] We cannot be sure exactly what Rebiba objected to. But we do know what changes were made in the text when it was revised and reprinted at Venice in 1578 after the Venetian Inquisitor Marco Medici, O.P., had gone over the Paris text, dropped a few passages he found offensive and made minor additions.[33] The changes made in the Venetian edition of the *De officio episcopi* are highlighted in our edition, but we must not forget that the *De officio episcopi* was only one of many works in the Paris edition, some of which touched more delicate subjects.

The basic Latin text printed here is based on that in the first edition of Contarini's works, *Opera* (Paris: Apud Sebastianum Nivellium, 1571), pp. 401-431. But as pointed out above, Cardinal Rebiba tried to block the sale of the edition until it had been corrected. The two subsequent editions of the *Opera* were published by the presses of Aldo Manuzio (1578) and Damiano Zenario (1589).[34] The two Venetian editions are identical and contain the corrections made by Medici or his assistants. The passages printed here in italics

---

[31] Ibid., 344-345.

[32] Ibid., 343 and footnote 100.

[33] Fragnito, DBI 28, 190; Fragnito, *Gasparo Contarini,* 80-81.

[34] Why did Alvise Contarini choose these publishers? Paris and Venice were the two largest printing centers in Europe. The printing firm of Sébastien Nivelle was noted for its Catholic orthodoxy (see Fragnito, *Gasparo Contarini,* 359). More important, Alvise was Venetian ambassador to France from 1569 to 1572 and hence in a position to see his uncle's work through the press at Paris. The Aldine Press was the most distinguished in Italy and was located at Venice where Alvise had returned and held public office in 1578. He also wrote a work on Venetian history in fourteen books which remains in manuscript.

were dropped in the Venetian editions. Partly to cover the transitions made by these omissions and partly to stress Contarini's orthodoxy the Venetian editions contain several short insertions; these are printed in decorated brackets { }. The page numbers of the printed editions are printed here in square brackets [ ].

The footnotes to the Latin text give all the corrections found in the two manuscripts which I examined that change the meaning of Contarini's text, however slightly. I have not noted minor stylistic changes, which are usually mere shifts in word order. Our edition does not pretend to be a critical text, for that would have involved collating all the extant manuscripts of Contarini and indicating even the smallest stylistic variations. The two manuscripts I have examined are both from the Biblioteca Vaticana. One is Cod. Vat. Lat. 11526, ff. 4-53, and is designated here by V in the notes; interestingly, it belonged to Cardinal Gianpietro Carafa.[35] The other is Cod. Ottob. Lat. 897, ff. 3-33; it is here designated by O in the footnotes. Its title page states "ex codicibus Joannis Angeli, Ducis ab Altaemps." Since the most important difference between the manuscripts and printed editions was an omitted passage which was too long to put in the footnotes, I have printed it with a translation as an appendix at the end of the text.[36]

As an introduction I have added the letter which Gasparo Contarini addressed to Pietro Lippomano when he sent Lippomano the text of his work; it is not found in the printed editions of Contarini's works but has been printed by Fragnito.[37] The letter gives some information about the reason why Contarini wrote his

---

[35] Fragnito, *Gasparo Contarini*, 82n.

[36] This long passage is printed by Fragnito, *Gasparo Contarini*, 209-211. She also points out most of the significant omissions and corrections in the text that I have noted. It is at her advice that I consulted the Vatican manuscripts, and I have been able to make some minor additions to her work.

The omitted passage is an attack on popular devotions which Contarini regards as superstitious; he argues that Christian faith should be centered on God and Christ rather than devotion to various patron saints. He also attacks the rivalry among religious orders. The good bishop must suppress tricksters who peddle semi-pagan devotions to ignorant peasants. Contarini's attack has an Erasmian ring which would have been quite acceptable among high churchmen of the Renaissance but was less so during the Counter Reformation when the passage seemed to echo Protestant attacks on popular Catholicism.

[37] Ibid., 207-209. It is found in Cod. Ottob. Lat. 897 but not in Cod. Vat. Lat. 11526.

treatise; its florid flattery is typical of Renaissance letters of dedication. Contarini does refer to Lippomano's youth but tries to put a positive twist on this by comparing Lippomano to the young David whom God promised in the Psalms to help. In his letter Contarini apologizes for his pedestrian Latin style, which he blames on his devotion to studying Aristotle and the medieval scholastics. In fact his writing is bland and sometimes murky, but his study of Aristotle and Aquinas did have one good effect on his writing: clear organization in presenting his ideas.

There is evidence that the Venetian printers had access to a manuscript since they added a few words found in the manuscripts but not in the Paris edition.[38] Scholars interested in investigating additional Contarini manuscripts should consult Paul Oskar Kristeller's classic *Iter Italicum*.[39]

Footnotes to the Latin text indicate variant readings found in the manuscripts which were consulted. Notes to the English translation provide explanations and document Contarini's quotations and references.

Contarini's text, aside from being divided into two books, contains no paragraphs or internal divisions whatever. I have divided the text and translation into paragraphs to ease the task of readers. His sentences sometimes begin with capital letters, sometimes not: here I have not modified his text. Like most Renaissance authors writing in Latin, he begins most sentences with a connective: thus in the first paragraph of Book I we find *etenim, vero, Nam, tamen,* and *enim* as the first or second word of a sentence. Modern English makes far less use of such connectives so I have often omitted many of them in the translation. I have also broken up many of Contarini's longer sentences for easier reading. Contarini refers to the Bible seventeen times; I have provided my own translation for his four short quotations from the Bible.

---

[38] For example, {inquam} is found on p. 403 of the Venice editions but is not found on the same page of Paris edition. It is found in the Vat. Lat. manuscript. It is obvious that the Venetian printers mainly worked from the Paris edition since all three printed editions have the same pagination, which the Venetian had to work hard to keep even though they had dropped material from the Paris edition.

[39] Fragnito discusses various manuscripts, *Gasparo Contarini*, 82-83n.

SELECTED BIBLIOGRAPHY

The bibliography on Contarini is very large; readers who want a more comprehensive bibliography should consult Elisabeth Gleason's recent biography of Contarini and Gigliola Fragnito's "Bibliografia contariniana" in the Cavazzana Romanelli volume listed below (pp. 255-66). The bibliography here tries to identify the most important books and articles for the study of Contarini and his book on the duty of a bishop, especially works available in English.

Cavazzana Romanelli, Francesca, ed. *Gaspare Contarini e il suo tempo: atti convegno di studio*. Venice: Comune di Venezia, Assessorato Affari Istituzionali, and Studium Cattolico Veneziano, 1988.

Dittrich, Franz. *Gasparo Contarini, 1483-1542: Eine Monographie*. Braunsberg, 1885.

Fragnito, Gigliola. "Aspetti della censura ecclesiastica nell' Europa della Controriforma: l'edizione parigiana delle opere di Gasparo Contarini." *Rivista di storia e letteratura religiosa* 21 (1985): 3-48.

_____. "Cultura umanistica e riforma religiosa: il 'De officio boni viri ac probi episcopi' di Gasparo Contarini." *Studi veneziani* 11 (1969): 75-189.

_____. *Gasparo Contarini: un magistrato veneziano al servizio della cristianità*. Florence: Olschki, 1988. This reprints both the articles listed above.

_____. *Memoria individuale e construzione biografica. Beccadelli, Della Casa, Vettori alle origini di un mito*. Urbino: Argalia Editore, 1978. A study of the first two biographies of Contarini.

Gilbert, Felix. "Religion and Politics in the Thought of Gasparo Contarini" in *Action and Conviction in Early Modern Europe*. Edited by T. K. Rabb and J. E. Seigel. Princeton: Princeton University Press, 1969.

Gleason, Elisabeth G. *Gasparo Contarini: Venice, Rome, and Reform*. Berkeley: University of California Press, 1993.

Jedin, Hubert, and Giuseppe Alberigo. *Il tipo ideale di vescovo secondo la riforma cattolica*. Brescia: Morcelliana, 1985.

Logan, Oliver. "The Ideal Bishop and the Venetian Patriciate: c. 1430- c. 1630." *Journal of Ecclesiastical History* 29 (1978): 415-50.

_____. *The Venetian Upper Clergy in the 16th and Early 17th Centuries: A Study of Religious Culture.* Lewiston: Edwin Mellen Press, 1996.

Matheson, Peter. *Cardinal Contarini at Regensburg.* Oxford: Clarendon Press, 1972.

Minnich, Nelson H., and Elisabeth G. Gleason. "Vocational Choices: An Unknown Letter of Pietro Querini to Gasparo Contarini and Niccolò Tiepolo (April, 1512)." *Catholic Historical Review* 75 (1989): 1-20.

Olin, John, ed. *The Catholic Reformation: Savonarola to Ignatius Loyola.* New York: Harper and Row, 1969.

Piton, M. "L'idéal épiscopal selon les prédicateurs français de la fin du XVᵉ siècle au début du XVIᵉ, *Revue d'historie ecclésiastique* 41 (1966) 77-118, 393-423.

Ross, James Bruce. "The Emergence of Gasparo Contarini: A Bibliographical Essay." *Church History* 41 (1972): 1-24.

_____. Gasparo Contarini and His Friends." *Studies in the Renaissance* 17 (1970): 192-232.

Rückert, Hanns. *Die theologische Entwicklung Gasparo Contarinis.* Arbeiten zur Kirchengeschichte. Bonn: A. Marcus und E. Weber, 1926.

Tellechea Idigoras, Jose Ignacio. *El Obispo ideal en el siglo de la Reforma.* Rome: Iglesia nacional española, 1963.

Tramontin, Silvio. "Il 'De officio episcopi' di Gaspare Contarini." *Studia Patavina* 12 (1965): 292-303.

THE OFFICE
OF A
BISHOP

DE OFFICIO VIRI BONI
ET PROBI EPISCOPI

Reverendissimo in Christo Patri Petro Lippomano Episcopo Bergomati electo. Gaspar Contarenus Foelicitatem.[1]

Si mearum voluissem habere virium rationem, Reverendissme Praesul, haud sane tam facile persuaderi mihi potuisset ut ad te de officio boni viri ac probi episcopi aliquid unquam conscriberem. Nam mihi ipse sum conscius christianae disciplinae eruditionem in me admodum exiguam esse, ut taceam de eloquentiae studiis ac universo orationis ornatu, a quibus iam a prima adolescentia abductus ad studia philosophiae barbaris auctoribus conscripta, omnem fere in his aetatem consumpsi; quare effectum est ut desuetudine latinae lectionis nullum prope ornatum ac elegantiam oratio nostra adepta sit, sed pro ea induerit barbaram quandam faciem, eam videlicet quam ex auctoribus illis barbaris contraxisse par erat. Nihil vero tibi mittendum esse noveram quod ad rerum ac sententiarum gravitatem non omni ex parte excultum esset. Nam praeterquam quod in studiis pontificii iuris iam aliquot annos maxima cum laude in Bononiensi Gymnasio versari, adeo es in latinis literis ac in dicendi ratione eruditus ut vel doctissimorum ac in latinae linguae peritissimorum hominum oratio iudicium tuum non immerito vereri debeat. Verum has omnes rationes vicit unica benevolentiae ac amicitiae nostrae necessitudo quae potius ut inepti notam subirem mihi persuadebat, quam ut voluntati tuae ac amicis precibus non satisfacerem.

Considerabam enim te cum primum a Summo Pontifice in Episcopum Bergomatem adscitus es, enixissime id a me per literas contendisse meque haud cogitantem an solvendo forem, nescio [3v] quodam spiritu ac numine impellente, et id tibi praestiturum pollicitum fuisse, et divinante quodammodo animo id agere coepisse primis statim literis quibus tibi sum gratulatus per egregia atque summa episcopatus dignitate tibi collata, quae certe cum divinitus evenisse cogitarem. Sperare coepi orationi nostrae, quamvis incultae ac ineruditae, divina ope non defuturam fortasse vim quandam quae animum tuum monere posset. Augebat hanc spem nostram tua erga

[1] Bibliotheca vaticana, Codex Ottob. Lat. 897, ff. 3r-4r.

ON THE DUTY OF A GOOD MAN
AND UPRIGHT BISHOP

Gasparo Contarini [sends] greetings to the most reverend in Christ Pietro Lippomano, Bishop Elect of Bergamo.

If I had wanted to take into account my own abilities, Reverend Prelate, it surely would not have been so easy to persuade me ever to write you anything on the duty of a good man and upright bishop. I am aware how very tiny is my knowledge of Christian formation—to say nothing about rhetorical studies and all elegance in discourse, for from my early adolescence I was shifted from them to studying philosophical works written by barbarian authors and spent almost all my years in them. That has resulted in our style having acquired very little eloquence and elegance due to rustiness in reading Latin; instead it has put on a certain barbarian appearance, namely that normally picked up from those barbarian authors. I was aware that nothing should be sent you unless all its parts had been crafted to the seriousness of the subject and content. For besides the fact that you have devoted several years to the study of pontifical law with the highest praise at the University of Bologna, you are so learned in Latin letters and the art of speaking that even men who are very learned and skilled in the Latin tongue have good reason to be fearful about your judgment on their discourse. But the singular pressure of our goodwill and friendship has overcome all these reasons and persuaded me that I should rather risk my being accounted foolish than fail to satisfy your wish and kind requests.

I took into consideration that when the supreme pontiff first approved you as Bishop of Bergamo you urged this on me most earnestly by letter. I promised to provide you with it, pushed forward by some spirit or holy impulse and hardly thinking about whether I would carry through. I began working on it with a certain prophetic spirit right away in the first letters by which I congratulated you for the outstanding and supreme dignity of the episcopacy conferred upon you—something I thought had certainly happened very providentially. I began to hope that our discourse, however inelegant and unlearned, by divine help perhaps might not lack a certain power which could instruct your heart. Your goodwill toward me and our

me ac res nostras benevolentia iam pridem mihi perspecta, in qua plurimum esse virium arbitrabar, ut tibi neque ingratae, neque inutiles futurae res nostrae essent, qualescumque tales forent. Dedi igitur operam ut per me cum ex morali philosophia, tum maxime ex christiana disciplina praecepta cogerentur in unum quibus et vir bonus et probus episcopus in officio contineri queat. Qua in re diligentiam adhibuimus, neglecto interim orationis ornatu, ut brevi, non obscura tamen oratione totum hoc negotium absolverem. Nam deterrere lectorem obscura solent, prolixa vero tedio afficere. Contraximus ergo, servata perspicuitate quantum potuimus, opus nostrum ac in duo volumina distinximus quorum priore animum viri ac episcopi probi formavimus virtutibus ac moralibus et christianis ac generalia quaedam praecepta adiunximus; posteriore vero perstrinximus omnia fere singillatim officia, quae praestare oportere episcopum duximus hisce virtutibus praeditum atque ornatum. In animo fuerat tertium quoque volumen subicere in quo plurimorum praesulum christianorum priscae aetatis exemplis omnis institutio prioribus voluminibus a nobis expressa confirmaretur. Id namque reliquum videbatur, nam in quacumque functione imitatione insignium virorum ingenui cuiusque animus maxime [4r] excitari consuevit. Caeterum cum propter occupationes quasdam familiares non possem satis commode huiusmodi exempla ex christianis monumentis conquirere teque nossem huiusce generis auctorum valde studiosum esse, omnem hanc operam in te reieci.

Accipe ergo quantulumcumque sit amici munus in quo, si non aliud quod eximium sit, propensionem tamen animi nostri cognosces. In primis vero enitere ne eam expectationem quam omnes ferme de te conceperunt, aliqua in parte defraudes. Nos certe ita de te speramus idque ex multis coniectamus te hac nostra tempestate in aetate admodum iuvenili, quemadmodum David, a Domino electum esse ut gregem suum pascas et priscae christianorum virtutis exempla renoves, quod quamvis difficillimun sit, facile tamen praestabis divina ope adiutus, dummodo tibi ipse non desis. Putato namque id tibi ex psalmis dictum esse: "Inveni David servum meum, oleo sancto meo unxi eum, nihil proficiet inimicus in eo, manus enim mea auxiliabitur

endeavors, which had long before been evident to me, increased this hope of ours; I considered that your goodwill would be so powerful that our endeavors, however they turned out, would be neither unwelcome to you nor useless. Therefore I worked away so that through me the precepts from both moral philosophy and especially from Christian formation might be pulled together so that by them a good man and upright bishop could be made steadfast in his duty. On this point we have worked diligently, meanwhile disregarding eloquent discourse, so that I might carry out this whole task in a short but not obscure discourse. For obscure [books] usually turn off the reader but long-winded ones cause boredom. As much as we could while retaining clarity, we have narrowed our work and divided it into two books; in the first of them we have molded the heart of the upright man and bishop with moral and Christian virtues, and we have added some general precepts. In the second book we touch upon individually almost all the duties which we judged a bishop graced and endowed with these virtues ought to perform. I had in mind to add a third book which would reaffirm by the examples of many Christian prelates of early times all the training which we discussed in the previous books. It seemed a good legacy, for in any sort of role the heart of a worthy person is wont to be enormously encouraged by imitating outstanding men. But due to certain family preoccupations I was unable to investigate in sufficient detail examples from the Christian memoirs, and since I knew that you are very interested in authors of this sort, I turned this whole task over to you.

Accept then this small gift of a friend; in it, if it is not something special, you can still recognize the inclination of our heart. Strive especially lest you in some way fall short of that expectation which almost everybody has formed about you. We certainly hope this from you, and for many [reasons] we have expected this: that God has chosen you during this our time at a very young age, like David, to feed his flock and to renew the examples of the pristine virtue of Christians. Although this may be very difficult, still you will easily carry it out helped by divine aid, provided that you do not fall short of yourself. Regard as addressed to you what is said in the Psalms, "I have found David my servant, I have anointed him with my holy oil, his enemy will succeed at nothing against him, for my hand will

ei." Ne dubita ergo, mi praesul, bono animo christianum episcopum age, christianum, inquam, idest non ambitiosum, non voluptatibus emancipatum, non avarum, non segnem ac desidem, denique non lupum, sed verum tui gregis pastorem, cuius interest non tantum opes, ac commoda, verum etiam animam suam, idest, vitam suam ponere pro ovibus suis, ut inquit Christus in evangelio. Sciasque te in christiana religione ex episcopatus dignitate non tam perfectam vitam profiteri, idest, eam qua ad perfectionem tenditur qualem monachi profitentur, sed eam perfectam vitam qua quis iam perfectus sit aliosque valeat ad perfectionem deducere. Vide quod professus fueris, nunc considera quid praestare debeas. Verum ne in praefatione ea monere te videar quae me collegisse in opuscolo nostro supra dixeram finem hic faciam. Tu caetera in libello leges. Vale ac tui me observantissimum ama.

LIBER PRIMUS

Deus optimus universitatis rerum conditor, sapientissimusque naturae institutor, duplici via, tum res, quae oculis subiectae sunt, atque sensu comprehendi queunt, tum etiam illas, quae cuiusque sensus facultatem excedunt, ad propriam perfectionem deducit. non nullae etenim ductui naturae obtemperantes, suos quaeque attingunt fines, nullo rationis, aut electionis usu adhibito. Res vero mentis compotes tali natura instituit, ut se ipsis quodammodo ducibus, rationis seu electionisque usu, ad illam, quae debetur eis, perfectionem devenirent. qua in re excellentiori modo similitudinem suam in rationali natura expressit, quam in rationis experte. Nam quemadmodum ipsi sibi perfectio est, neque alicui foelicitatem suam acceptam refert; pari quoque ratione, pro earum naturae modo, rationales naturas voluit sibi ut essent perfectionis auctores: quod tamen nequaquam fieri ab-

come to his aid."[1] So don't hesitate, my prelate; play the Christian bishop with a happy heart—Christian I say—that is, not ambitious, not given over to pleasure, not greedy, not sluggish or lazy, and finally not a wolf but your flock's true shepherd, whose concern is to lay down not just his wealth and convenience but even his soul, that is his life, for his sheep, as Christ says in the gospel.[2] May you also realize that in the Christian religion because of the dignity of the episcopacy you do not profess a perfect life, that is, one which aims at the kind of perfection monks profess, but that perfect life by which one is already perfect and is able to lead others to perfection.[3] See what you will have professed; now reflect on how you should carry it out. But lest I seem to be admonishing you in the preface about what I have said above in our little work, I will make an end here. You can read the rest in the book. Farewell and love me, who greatly respects you.

BOOK I

God, who is the good creator of everything in the universe and the wise author of nature, leads down a twofold path to their specific perfection both the things which are observable by the eye and are capable of being grasped by the senses and those things which transcend the faculty of any sense. Some things, obeying the lead of nature, attain their own ends without employing any use of reason or choice. Things capable of mental activity, however, he made to be of such a nature that by using their reason and their ability to choose they may somehow by their own guidance come to that perfection which befits them. In this regard he expresses his own image to a higher degree in a rational nature than in one lacking reason. For just as he is his own perfection, and he does not look to someone else for the happy estate which is his own, so too in like manner he willed that rational natures, according to the measure of their nature, would be the authors of their own perfection—but this is in no way to be

---

[1] Ps 89:21.

[2] John 10:11.

[3] Members of religious orders, because they took vows of poverty, chastity and obedience which were traditionally linked to the counsels of perfection, were said to be in a state of perfection in the sense of striving for perfection. Bishops, who outranked religious, were regarded as belonging to the order of perfection attained— regardless of their personal moral and spiritual performance. Here Contarini seems to depend on Thomas Aquinas, *Summa Theologiae*, II-II, 184, 6-7.

sque eius influentia putandum est. nihil enim principis illius cau-
sae ordinem evadit; cum irrationalia alieno veluti impulsu suis quaeque
finibus potiantur.

Hae vero rationales naturae, quae suis quodammodo auspiciis,
optatum a naturaque insitum finem adipiscuntur, sunt duplices.
quaedam enim omnino corporum sunt immunes, quales sunt Angeli:
contra aliae corporeis rebus affines, quae non nisi corporibus
coniunctae a primo illo omnium auctore in lucem prodeunt, rationales hominum animi {sunt}. Horum utrisque duo fines, duplexque
perfectio debetur. quorum alterum assequi queunt innatis viribus,
atque naturali facultate. Alterum vero nequaquam adipisci possunt
absque peculiari quadam ope, privatim sibi divinitus allata. prior finis, posteriori hoc longe inferior; verum praeparatio quaedam existit
ad posteriorem adipiscendum. Angeli multo excellentiorem in rerum hac universitate gradum sortiti quam homines, in primo statim
rerum exordio sunt assecuti naturalem atque inchoatam, quam supra
dixi, perfectionem: simulque gratiam sunt adepti, quae tanquam
seminarium quoddam est perfectissimae atque excellentissimae illius
foelicitatis; ad quam paulo post hi evecti sunt, qui a supremo bonorum
omnium fonte non aversi, in eo potius, quam in se [402] foelices esse
voluerunt.

Hominum vero natura, quoniam ab angelica perfectione distat,
multum temporis multumque sudoris impendit in illa foelicitate
consequenda: perfectam autem nequaquam attingit in hac mortali
vita; verum post mortem qui sancte pieque vixere divino numine ad
eam evehuntur. satis vero habent, si donec mortalem vitam in terris
agunt, Christianis virtutibus praeter eas quas morales dicimus,
excolunt animum, quibus veluti catenis ac vectibus trahuntur ad
supremum foelicitatis gradum. Sed quoniam homo solus nequaquam
sufficit ad ea sibi comparanda, quae pro tuendo corpore necessaria
sunt, nedum beatitudinem per se acquirat; effectum est, ut homines
simul viverent in civili societate, in qua alter alterius ope, tum
politicam, tum etiam Christianam adipisceretur perfectionem: ut non
tantum propter liberam eligendi vim, sed etiam propter operam
vicissim praestitam sibi ipsis essent perfectionis ac foelicitatis esse
auctores. caeterum, quia unusquisque maxime suum aut familiae
bonum procurat, opus fuit ut commune bonum alicui demandaretur.

thought of as taking place without his influence. For nothing escapes the order of that first cause, since all irrational beings obtain their ends by a sort of outside impulse.

But these rational natures, which somehow under their own guidance attain the end which they desire and which nature has put within them, are of two types. Some are entirely free of bodies, such as are the angels. On the other hand {there are} other things that share in the status of bodily objects; these are the rational human souls, which come forth into the light from that first author of all things in no wise other than as conjoined to bodies. Both of these possess two ends and a twofold perfection. They can attain one of them by their innate powers and natural ability. But they absolutely cannot achieve the other unless a certain special help is divinely bestowed on them individually. The first end is far inferior to this second one, but it serves as a preparation of sorts for obtaining the second one. Angels have been allotted a far higher level than men in this universe of things; right from the first origin of things the [angels] achieved a natural and preliminary perfection, as I said above. At the same time they also received a grace which is a sort of seedbed for the most perfect and excellent happiness; those who do not rebel against the supreme font of all good things but chose to be happy in him rather than in themselves were soon after lifted up to this happiness.

But human nature, because it falls short of angelic perfection, expends much time and much laborious effort in attaining that happiness. In no way does it achieve perfect happiness in this mortal life, but after death divine power carries up to [happiness] those who have lived holy and devout lives. It is enough for them if, while they are leading their mortal life on earth, they perfect their soul with the Christian virtues besides those we call the moral [virtues]; by these as by chains and pulleys they are carried to the highest level of happiness. But since man alone is utterly incapable of obtaining for himself the things which he needs to protect his body, so too he is even less able to acquire happiness by himself. The result is that men live together in a civil society in which they achieve both political and also Christian perfection by helping one another, so that not only because of their power of free choice but also because of their working together with one another they are the authors of their own perfection and happiness. Moreover, since each person looks chiefly after his own good and that of his family, there was need that the common good be

quod, cum in communione quadam civilis coetus praecipue consistat, melius mandatur uni, quam pluribus. Hinc civitatibus atque populis Reges atque Episcopi praesident. Regum officium praecipuum est, ut cives bona civitatis institutione probos reddant, eosque evehant qui natura capaces sunt ad *contemplativam* {politicam} usque foelicitatem. Horum gratia, externorum bonorum copiam, militaremque potentiam civitati, cui praesunt, nituntur omnibus viribus comparare.

Episcopus autem altiorem quendam scopum praescriptum habet. Nam fidei suae commissam civitatem Christianis institutionibus, divinisque legibus erudiendam, atque in officio continendam suscipit; susceptamque ad supremam eam foelicitatem dirigit omni conatu; quam sine Christiana pietate atque institutione sperare stultum, simulque nefarium est. quo fit, ut longe maiori dignitate Episcopus praeditus esse censeri debeat, quam princeps civitatis. Hic namque curam habet humanae foelicitatis, quae dispositio quaedam est ad Christianas virtutes supremamque *illam* beatitudinem; quarum ducem, ac magistrum Episcopum esse diximus. ita fit, ut utrunque oporteat excellenti quodam animo esse, omnibusque virtutibus ornato. primum quoniam natura comparatum est, ut unumquodque efficiens similem sibi effectum pariat; forma enim et natura propria rei, quae agit, actionis principum est; ex quo efficitur, ut guberator ac princeps, qualis ipse fuerit, talem efficiat civitatem. bonam ergo et beatam nequaquam reddet is guberator qui non tali ipse quoque habitu praeditus fuerit. Huc adde, quod in his quae ad mores pertinent, unusquisque facta potius monitoris sectatur, quam verba; tumque sibi vere dari verba a praecipiente credit, si secus vivat, ac vivendum esse aliis praecipiat. postremo, ut inquit Plato, praefectus civitatis talem in urbe Reipublicae institutionem facit, qualem prius in animi sui Republica gesserit.

entrusted to somebody. Since a civil group consists mainly in a certain mutual sharing, this is better entrusted to one person rather than many. Hence kings and bishops have charge over states and nations. The main task of kings is to make the citizens upright by the good administration of the city and to elevate up to even a *contemplative* {political} happiness those who have the natural capacity for it. For the sake of these they strive with all their powers to obtain an abundance of temporal goods and military power for the city over which they preside.

The bishop, however, has a certain higher goal assigned him. For he undertakes to educate the city entrusted to him in Christian teaching and divine laws and to keep it to its duty. By his every effort he directs [the city] he has received to that supreme happiness, which it is senseless and likewise wicked to hope for without Christian piety and instruction. Thus it happens that the bishop should be credited as being endowed with a far greater dignity than the city's prince. For the latter has care of human happiness, which is a sort of predisposition toward Christian virtues and toward *that* supreme happiness, of all of which, as we have said, the bishop is the leader and teacher. Thus it happens that both should possess a certain splendid spirit adorned with all the virtues. First because nature has ordained that every efficient cause brings forth an effect like itself, for the form and the specific nature of the thing that acts are the source of the action. From this it follows that a governor or prince produces a city like to himself. That governor will not reproduce a good and happy [city] who himself has not also been endowed with the same characteristics. Add to this that in matters which pertain to conduct, everybody imitates the deeds rather than the words of his teacher; moreover he believes that he is really being given mere words by his preceptor if the latter lives otherwise than he teaches others to live. Finally, as Plato said, the head of the state establishes in his city the kind of government that he has already formed in the republic of his own soul.[4]

---

[4] Central to Plato's *Republic* is the argument that the relationship among powers of the soul resemble types of government. The argument begins in Book II (368C-369A), reappears in Book IV (427C-444A), and returns again in Book IX (588B-591E). The intelligent man "keeps his gaze fixed on the *politeia* within him and guards against disturbing anything in it" (IX, 591E). Contarini follows Plato in distinguishing three parts to the soul: the appetitive, the spirited or *pars irascibilis*, and the rational part (Book IV, 435C-442C).

Nam in quovis homine ex irascibli concupiscibilique animae partibus, atque ex rationali, veluti quaedam Respublica constituitur. si quis ergo ita vivit, ut eius appetitus a virtutibus non deflectant,[2] solamque rationem ducem in quacunque actione [403] sequantur; optimam hic in animo suo constituit Reipublicae formam, et eam ex qua in civitatem derivetur optimatium, seu probi principis principatus, at si irascibilis animi vis ambitione, aut huiusmodi quopiam morbo affecta, imperium in animum nostrum exerceat, ipsique caetera pareant quae in homine sunt, ambitiosam aut militarem gubernationis formam, in populo atque urbe, cui praeest, statim parit. sin vero libido, aut avaritia, caeteraeque concupiscilibis partis aegritudines, ac pestes aliis omnibus praestiterint, hinc popularis, ac tandem tyrannica civitas efficitur, cum maximo civium omnium detrimento. quamobrem civitatis principem, christianique gregis pastorem maxime decet, ut quam optimam animi Rempublicam intra se gerant, si recte civitatem sint administraturi, atque ad optatam beatitudinem pro viribus perducturi.

longe tamen maior animi perfectio in Episcopo requiritur, quam in principe: tum quia ad supremum quendam finem atque excellentissimis virtutibus Christianis {inquam} populus, cuius curam gerit, est ipsi instituendus: tum etiam quod cum unusquisque tanto oneri ferendo per se sit impar, purgatissimo animo eum esse oportet, atque ad divinas illuminationes suscipiendas idoneo, qui se tam magnae provinciae accingit. Nam cum egregio miroque ordine hanc rerum universitatem supremus ille artifex moderetur, inferioraque superioribus, veluti quibusdam instrumentis, perducat ad proprios naturalesque fines; hunc tamen ordinem maxime praestat in humano genere dirigendo, ad aeternam illam foelicitatem, quo fit ut Angelis utatur tanquam ministris ad purgandas illustrandasque hominum mentes: obscurius tamen id praestat in his qui aliorum imperio et moderationi subiecti sunt; clarissme vero ac lucidissime in illis qui aliis curandis praesunt, dummodo sibi ipsi non desint, ipsumque humanum genus supremae huius beatitudinis quodammodo sibi auctor esse velit.

Episcopus autem medius est inter divinos spiritus, et humanum genus. ex quo perspicuum est, oportere Episcopum tum

---

[2] Here the printed editions follow O 6r; V 6v has, "Si quis, quodsi utriusque appetitus perturbationesque virtutibus moderatae, solamque rationem" etc.

For something like a republic is set up in each person on the basis of the soul's irascible and concupiscible parts and that of the rational [part]. If anybody lives so that his appetites do not turn aside from the virtues but follow reason alone as their leader in any action, that man has set up the best form of a republic in his soul and one from which the rulership of an aristocracy or of an upright prince flows into the city. But if the power of the irascible soul, influenced by ambition or any other similar sickness, holds sway in our soul, the other things which are in man yield to it; it immediately produces a popularity-seeking and military form of government in the people or city over which it has charge. But if passion or greed and the other sicknesses and plagues of the concùpiscible part of the soul gain control over everything else, there results a demagogic and finally a tyrannical city, to the extreme detriment of all the citizens. Therefore it is very fitting for the prince of the city and the pastor of Christian flock to govern the best possible republic of the soul within themselves if they are going to administer the city rightly and guide [it] to the desired happiness with their whole strength.

But a bishop needs a far greater perfection of soul than does a prince, both because he has the task of educating the people, {I say}, over whom he has care, in outstanding Christian virtues for a certain supreme end and also because, since any individual is unequal by himself to carrying such a burden, he who girds himself for so large a task ought have a soul completely cleansed and suited for receiving divine enlightenment. For that supreme Artisan guides this universe of things with outstanding and wondrous order and leads to their proper and natural ends lesser things by higher things, as if by certain instruments. He best manifests that order, however, in guiding the human race to everlasting happiness. Thus it happens that he uses the angels as his instruments in cleansing and enlightening human minds. He provides this more secretly among those who are subject to the control and guidance of others, but very clearly and openly in those who are in charge of caring for others, provided only that they themselves should not be remiss and that the human race should wish itself somehow to be the author of this supreme happiness.

The bishop, however, finds himself placed between the divine spirits and the human race. From this it is clear that the bishop should

angelicae, tum humanae naturae quadam ratione participem esse; quod cum de se nullus, quanquam virtutibus ornatissimus, polliceri possit; iccirco Episcopatum optare absque arrogantiae crimine, aut avaritiae, aut ambitionis, nequit ullus. absque ullo tamen crimine quisque optare potest, eam sibi divinitus animi excellentiam concedi, ut gerendo Episcopatui idoneus haberi possit: ad eam tamen dignitatem nequaquam accedendum est, nisi vocatis a Deo, et a summo Pontifice cooptatis, absque ullo ipsorum ambitu; quemadmodum a Moyse Aaron fratrem ad sacerdotium vocatum legimus. ex his igitur nemo, quamvis tardus ingenio, non perspicere potest, quanta animi perfectione atque excellentia preditus is ipse esse debeat, quem diximus oportere supra humanam sortem, ad Angelicae usque naturae participationem extolli. Caeterum, quoniam ad tam magnum animi profectum non nisi quibusdam veluti gradibus pervenitur, nos quoque ordinemur a levioribus, pedetentimque accedemus ad sublimiora: idque prius generali quadam figura ac ratione; postmodum vero in specie magis.

Principio ergo, qui Episcopatui gerendo dignus [404] haberi vult, aciem mentis intendat, ut in unaquaque actione quod honestum ac decorum sit intueri queat. multi sunt enim qui ad honesti splendorem vel nullos, vel lippientes oculos adferant. deinde tam vehementi amore erga honestum afficiatur, ut nullis illecebris voluptatum, nullaque alia animi perturbatione ab hoc honesti sensu possit abduci. verum quoniam honestum rationis quoddam est bonum, multaeque animi partes sunt rationis expertes, quas scilicet communes gerimus cum caeteris animantibus brutis: duae vero sunt appetitus vires, quae sensibilem animi partem comitantur: quarum alteram concupiscendi vim, alteram autem irascendi appellare consuevimus: Hae autem suapte natura rationis expertes sunt, neque appetunt honestum, quod rationis esse bonum supra diximus: in homine mentis compote, in quo naturali quodam ordine tum corpus animae paret, et ex imperio animae in quascunque movetur partes,[3] tum ratio caeteris animae facultatibus imperat: atque hae tamen partes, quas ratione carere diximus, nescio quonam pacto factae sunt ipsae quoque compotes

---

[3] Here both V 9r and O 7v insert the following: Atque et in eas ad quas moveri contra appetitionem naturalem corporis est in quantum terrestre corpus. Tum et ratio (quod primarium obtinuit) caeteris animae facultatibus imperat, hae etenim irrationales partes factae sunt ipse quoque compotes rationes quatenus ....

in some way share in both angelic and human nature. Nobody, however greatly adorned with virtues, can promise that about himself; for that reason nobody can desire episcopal rank without the sin of arrogance or avarice or ambition. But one can without any sin hope that he may be divinely granted such excellence of soul as to be accounted suitable for holding episcopal rank. Still such a dignity is not to be approached except by those who are called by God and ratified by the supreme pontiff, without any canvassing of their own, just as we read how Moses called his brother Aaron to the priesthood.[5] There is nobody, however slow of wit, who cannot see from these things how much perfection and excellence of soul a person ought to possess who, we have said, should be raised above the human condition even to participation in the angelic nature. Moreover, since one reaches to such a great progress of soul only, as it were, by certain upward stages, let us also begin with the easier stages and let us go forward step by step to the more sublime, doing so first by a certain general picture and account, but afterwards more in detail.

To start with, let the person who wants to be considered worthy of holding episcopal rank direct his mind's eye so that what is upright and dignified can be recognized in his every action. For there are many who turn either no glance or a bleary-eyed one toward the splendor of the honorable. Then let him be acted upon by such a powerful love for the honorable that he cannot be drawn away from this sense of the honorable by any allurements of pleasure or any other disquiet of soul. But what reason deems honorable is a sort of good, and many parts of the soul—namely those which we bear in common with the brute animals—are lacking in reason, for there indeed are two appetitive powers that accompany the sensitive part of the soul, one of which we are wont to call the concupiscible power and the other the irascible power, both of which by their very nature are lacking in reason and do not aspire toward the honorable, which we said above was the good of reason. In a man endowed with a mind, the body both obeys the soul by means of a certain natural ordering and is moved in its various parts by the command of the soul, and the reason gives orders to the other faculties of the soul. Nevertheless these parts, which we said lack reason, are in some mysterious way themselves also made capable of reason, namely insofar

[5] Heb 5:4.

rationis, quatenus scilicet naturali quodam nexu natae sunt menti obsequi, si interim paulatim assuescant nihil agere praeter rationalis partis imperium. Hoc vero nunquam commode praestare poterunt, nisi virtutes morales imbiberint, quibus ex[s]uperent naturae suae facultatem, et rationem quo vis pacto pertingant.

ex his ergo sic collectis efficitur, ut continuo ab ineunte aetate, qui probus Episcopus futurus sit, coercere has animi vires debeat, continereque intra limites a ratione praescriptas; atque his virtutibus excolere, quibus utranque excitari, ac rationem, honestique veluti quendam sensum adipisci, et ratione, et experimento compertum cuilibet potest esse. quam viam nisi fuerit ab adolescentia ingressus, in virili aetate constitutus, id aut nunquam, aut aegre praestabit. iuxta viam suam adolescens (inquit Salomon) cum senuerit non recedet ab ea. totis ergo viribus enitendum est, omnique conatu contendendum, ut a teneris annis, Herculis more, haec monstra molliamus ac perdomemus, atque assuefaciamus, ut iugum rationis pati in tenera aetate discant. Sed prius compescendae nobis erunt concupiscibilis animi perturbationes; quae et vehementissimae sunt, et in prima statim adolescentia bellum cient aduersus rationem acerrimum.

Haec igitur animi vis in illo aetatis lubrico temperantia est cohibenda: quae, si proprie sumatur, compescit ac coercet voluptates ex cibo potuque, atque ex venereis rebus emergentes: sed alio modo sumpta, late patet, atque avaritiam, invidentiam, et ambitionem, gravissimos animi morbos, expurgat. Quid enim est[4] liberalitas, nisi temperantia quaedam a nimia pecuniarum cupiditate, immoderataque largitione? aut quid aliud est ea virtus, quae cum sit circa mediocres honores, propria appellatione caret, nisi temperantia

---

[4] Here both V 10r and O 8r insert "per deos."

as they are born to obey the mind by some natural link if meanwhile they gradually become accustomed to doing nothing except by the command of the rational part. They could never have performed this appropriately unless they had imbibed the moral virtues by which they surpass the faculty of their nature and somehow reached out to reason.

These things thus brought together have the result that right from early adulthood the person who will be a good bishop ought to bring under control these powers of the soul and restrain them within the limits prescribed by reason. By reason and experiment anybody can discover how to develop in these virtues, how both [powers of the soul] can be stirred by them and how reason and a certain sense of the honorable can be acquired. He will either never or only barely distinguish himself unless starting from his youth he has established himself on this path during his young manhood. A person (Solomon says) will not depart from the path of his youth, even when he grows old.[6] Therefore we must struggle with all our powers and strive with a total effort that from our tender years, in the fashion of Hercules,[7] we soften up and tame these monsters and domesticate them so that they learn to bear the yoke of reason in their young manhood. But first we will have to bridle the unruly movements of the concupiscible soul; these are very strong and stir up the bitterest of wars against reason right from the start of adolescence.

Therefore this power of the soul during that slippery period of life is to be reined in by temperance, which, if rightly employed, bridles and checks the pleasures which flow from food, drink, and from sexual drives.[8] If it is employed in a different way, as is widely evident, it purges away greed, envy, and ambition—very serious sicknesses of the soul. For what is liberality, except a certain temperance against excessive desire for riches and immoderate spending? Or what is that other virtue (which lacks a specific name since it deals with minor honors) except a certain temperance from an

---

[6] Prov 22:6.

[7] The story of young Hercules at the crossroads debating whether to take the path of virtue or the path of pleasure is found in Cicero's *De Officiis*, I, 32, 118; it was a favorite theme of Petrarch and Coluccio Salutati and many Renaissance and Baroque painters. For modern studies on the Hercules theme, see Ronald G. Witt, *Hercules at the Crossroads: The Life, Works and Thought of Coluccio Salutati* (Durham: Duke University Press, 1983) 216.

[8] Confer St. Thomas Aquinas, *Summa Theologiae* (hence forward: S.T.) II-II, 142.

quaedam a nimia honoris cupiditate? indignatio quoque ab invidentia temperat, de qua infra cum de charitate disseremus. sunt etiam nonnulla concupiscibilis animi vitia, [405] quae hominum inter se consuetudinem maculant deterioremque faciunt.[5] Hic fictus atque adulator; ille urbanus aut scurra, contra quos morbos his pharmacis est utendum, ut veritate seu vivendi simplicitate, Christiano enim more loquar, simulationem omnem vitemus, affabilitate, turpes adulationes, atque importunas vel de minimis rebus contentiones: urbanitate et scurrilitatem, et consuetudinem agrestem ac morosam.

his non minus quam superioribus, temperantiae nomen accommodari potest. Nam et verus seu simplex, a quacunque temperat fictione, et affabilis a contentione, et urbanus, a scurrae verbis ac moribus. His ergo virtutibus concupiscibils anima est excolenda, ut discat rationem ducem in omnibus sequi, et ad quendam honesti sensum paulatim subduci consuescat, in nulla tamen animi perturbatione sedanda, magis est evitandum, in iuvenili praesertim aetate, quam in ea, quae ex ardore libidinis, illiusque voluptatis illecebris excitatur.

Haec enim omnium vehementissima est, maximeque "affigit humo divinae particulam aurae" (ut inquit Flaccus). qua in re considerandum erit, quam homine indignae sint eae voluptates, quibus in bruta animantia quodammodo degenerat; ante oculosque proponendum, quot celebres ac illustres viri res pulcherrime ab ipsis gestas, hac labe foedarint. maximaque cum ignominia tum superstites vixerint, tum etiam post obitum in memoria vulgi ore versentur, in quibus satis erit Salomonis sapientissimi ac potentissimi Regis exemplum; qui post multa praeclare ac magnifice gesta, tam turpiter, huiusce voluptatis illecebris captus, deflexit de via; ut ad idolatriae usque nefandissimum crimen collapsus fuerit; simulque abstinendum erit a consuetudine eorum quae animos iuvenum solent allicere ad huiusmodi voluptates, nec minus parcendum erit lectioni eorum auctorum, ac praesertim poetarum, qui amorum

---

[5] The last two words of this sentence are found neither in V 10r nor O 8r.

excessive desire for honor? Indignation restrains one from envy—more on this point later when we discuss charity. There are also several vices of the concupiscible soul, which stain and make worse the interaction of men with one another. This fellow is a phony and a flatterer; that fellow is a smooth operator or a dandy; against those sicknesses these medicines are to be used so that we shun all sham by the truth or simplicity of living—for I am speaking in a Christian manner; by affability [we shun] shameful flattery and insolent arguments even over trivial things; by urbanity [we shun] both buffoonery and a boorish and doleful manner.

The name of temperance can be adapted to these no less than the things [mentioned] above. For a true or straightforward person refrains from any fabrication, the affable man [refrains] from arguments, the urbane man [refrains] from the words and mannerisms of the dandy. The concupiscible soul is to be nurtured with these virtues so that it learns to follow reason as its leader in all things and grows accustomed gradually to being drawn to a certain sense of the honorable. But in calming the turmoil of the soul nothing is more to be avoided, especially at a youthful age, than that which is stirred up by the heat of lust and the enticements of that pleasure.

This is the most violent of all, and it does the most "to plunge into the earth the particle of the divine breath" (as Flaccus says).[9] On this subject it will be worth reflecting on how shameful in man are those pleasures by which he somehow descends to the level of the brute beasts. We should put before our eyes how many famous and distinguished men have befouled their splendid deeds by this stain. They both lived the rest of their lives in utter ignominy and after their death they also lived on in memory as a popular watchword. Among them the example of Solomon, a very wise and powerful king, will suffice; after many splendid and magnificent deeds, how shamefully he swerved from the path, captive to the enticements of this pleasure so that he fell right down into the most unspeakable sin of idolatry.[10] At the same time it will be necessary to steer clear of companionship with those women who make a practice of enticing the souls of the young men to such pleasures. It will be no less wrong to allow the reading of those authors, especially poets, who have left

[9] Horace, *Satires*, 2.2.79.
[10] 1 Kings 11:1-11.

monumenta posteris reliquerunt. qua in re non possum satis mirari nostrorum temporum consuetudinem, cum scilicet pueris (ut ita dixerim) vix bene natis, continuo legendos ac ediscendos, proponunt nonnullos poetarum libellos, amoribus ac libidinibus plenos; calcariaque addunt aetati, per se ad libidines sponte currenti. Nostrum vero Episcopum nollem ego a teneris annis hac vulgari ratione, sed potius secreta quadam ac diversa a vulgi consuetudine institutum fuisse. sin aliter, cum primum licebit, vellem ut ab huiusmodi poetarum studiis temperaret. sed nunc de his satis. inferius namque fusius dicturi sumus de Episcopi studiis. A crapula vero abstineat quantum fieri potest, nihil enim viro ingenuo indignius, quam ista ciborum ac potus ingluvies.

de liberalitate, quae sequitur, pauca quaedam nunc dicam; plura infra dicturus, cum de dispensatione redituum annuorum Episcopatus disseram. nunc id tantum monuisse sufficiat, nihil esse animi magis angusti, quam haec comparandarum pecuniarum sitis. miseranda profecto animarum aegritudo, qua homines usque eo obsequantur, ut vitae perfectionem, summumque bonum[6] ex divitiarum opibus sibi comparari posse existiment. sed ambitio, quae tota pendet ex vulgi errore, miserrima est: quam tamen differimus ad eum usque locum, in quo de magnanimitate dicemus. Verum cum homo non solus [406] vivat, sed aliorum quoque commercio utatur, dandum operae plurimum erit, ut iucundi amicis simus, caeterisque hominibus non ingrati. primum igitur observandum est, ut quam maxime fieri potest, in quacunque actione veritatem quandam (ut verbis Aristotelis utar), vel potius simplicitatem praestemus (ut Christiano more loquar). Haec animi virtus fictionem omnem, et in corporis gestu, atque habitu et in quacunque alia actione prorsus excludit; neque aliud ore praesefert aliud corde occultat. Rei namque simplicis unica quaedam

---

[6] In place of qua homines ... summumque bonum both V 12r and O 9r have the following: quae animo sui ipsius oblivionem adeo infundi ut perfectionem ipsum vitae sufficiens ex divitiarum opibus sibi comparari posse existimet ....

behind to posterity monuments to their love affairs. On this point I cannot be enough amazed at the practice of our times, namely when they propose for boys, who (if I may say so) have barely been born, the constant reading and study of several books of the poets full of loves and lusts.[11] They add a spur to an age which by itself runs willingly to lusts. I would not want our bishop to be brought up from his tender years in this common program but rather by a certain segregated and different [practice] than the common one. But if not that, as soon as it will be allowed, I would wish he would set limits to his studies in such poets. But enough on this for now. Below we will discuss the studies of the bishop at greater length. Let him abstain from drunkenness as far as possible, for nothing is more unworthy of a freeborn man than such gluttony in food and drink.

On liberality, the next topic, I will make some few remarks now;[12] I will say more below when I discuss the disposal of the annual income of the bishopric. For now let it be enough to have given only this warning: nothing characterizes a narrow mind more than this thirst for acquiring money. It is indeed the sort of terrible sickness of soul to which men yield to such a pitch that they think that from the wealth of riches they can acquire for themselves the perfection of life and the supreme good. But ambition, which is totally dependent on the mistaken view of the crowd, is utterly wretched; we, however, are putting off this subject until the place where we will discuss magnanimity. But since man does not live alone but uses dealings with others, we will have to try very hard to be affable with our friends and not unpleasant to other people. Therefore we should first observe that as far as at all possible in our every action we manifest a kind of truth in all our dealings (that I may use the words of Aristotle[13]), or rather a simplicity (that I may speak in a Christian manner). This virtue of the soul completely precludes all posturing both in our bodily carriage and bearing and in any other action. Nor does it put forth one thing with the mouth and hide another in the heart. For there is a certain unique, simple reality and the same com-

---

[11] Contarini doubtless had Catullus, Ovid, Propertius, and Martial in mind.

[12] Contarini's treatment of liberality parallels that of Aquinas, S.T., II-II, 117.

[13] Contarini does not seem to have a specific passage of Aristotle in mind here but merely wishes to contrast the mind and terminology of philosophers, centered on truth, and that of Christian writers, for whom virtues such as simplicity are the norm of conduct and reflect gospel values.

est, in quacunque eius parte, eademque habitudo. Nec etiam in conversatione hominum negligenda est iocunda quaedam affabilitas ac decora; ita ut neque adulationis crimine insimulari possimus, neque ulla morositate culpari: sed in convictu quoque hominum, ut simus faciles ac iocundi. pari ratione consuetudinis nobis utendum est, si quando iocosa incidunt; ad quae, animi reficiendi causa, plerunque homines divertunt, ut alacriores revertantur ad seria honestaque studia. in iocis ergo decorum quoddam servandum erit, ne videlicet videamur rustici, atque agrestes, neve contra scurrae ac mimi. sed condienda oratio erit urbanitate quadam ac lepore; ut simul faceta gravisque habeatur.Reprehendet aliquis fortasse diligentiam hac in parte nostram, quod potius civilem virum, quam Episcopum erudire videar. cui responsum velim, morales ac civiles virtutes, quamvis non ita Episcopi sint, ut aliis quoque non conveniant, quemadmodum nonnullae aliae, de quibus infra dicturi sumus, non tamen ab Episcopo putandum est alienas esse; quin potius fundamenta sunt quaedam, quibus sublatis, caeterae quoque Episcopo peculiares et propriae ruant necesse est. iccirco nobis, quibus tanquam ab incunabulis perfectum Episcopum erudire propositum fuit, nequaquam fuerunt omittendae.

Tempus nunc est, ut duram efferamque animi partem, irascendi inquam vim, non mollem quidem, sed constantem efficiamus. Huius praecipua virtus est fortitudo, qua firmamus molle illud animae atque effoeminatum, ne penitus subsidat ac defluat. Haec ea est virtus, quae virilitatem quandam, et robur animo praestat, omnibusque mortalibus, ac humanis rebus superiorem facit: in hac plus multo elucet decorum illud atque admirandum honesti, quam in quavis alia virtute: unde etiam sola per excellentiam quandam, virtutis nomen obstinuit apud veteres Romanos. circa mortis pericula, dolorumque tolerantiam maxime versatur haec virtus; in quibus ea potissimum ratione firmabimus animum, si constantissime tenebimus nihil honesto praeferendum esse, nullamque

portment in all one's dealings. Nor is a certain pleasant but dignified affability to be discounted in dealing with men, such that without it we could be charged with the fault of flattery or charged with any peevishness. Rather in our living together with men let us be easy-going and pleasant. We should take custom equally into account if humorous things pop up sometimes. Most men find diversion in these, for the sake of refreshing their soul, so that they may return more eagerly to serious and upright pursuits. A certain decorum should therefore be observed in jokes, lest we seem bumpkins or uncouth or, on the contrary, dandies or pranksters. Our speech is to be seasoned with a certain urbanity and pleasantness so that it attains wit and dignity at the same time.

Perhaps somebody will object to our diligence about this topic, because I may seem to be educating a citizen rather than a bishop. I would like to make this response to him: the moral and civic virtues should not be understood as being foreign to the bishop, even though they do not so much belong to the bishop that they do not also befit others, just like some other things we are going to talk about below. Rather there are certain fundamental things; if they are removed, the other [virtues] peculiar and specific to a bishop must also collapse. Hence we could by no means omit them, since we had set out to educate the perfect bishop as if from the crib.

It is now time for us to make the hard and savage part of the soul, the irascible power, I say, not indeed soft but steadfast. Its main virtue is the fortitude by which we firm up that soft and effeminate [part] of the soul, lest it wholly crouch down and slink away. This is the virtue which provides a certain manliness and strength to the soul; it makes one superior in all things mortal and human. In this virtue there shines forth the beauty and admirable character of an honorable person far more than any other virtue. Hence too this alone by means of a certain pre-eminence attained the name of virtue among the ancient Romans.[14] This virtue has its greatest role in [facing] the dangers of death and bearing sufferings; in these cases we will strengthen our soul mainly on the ground that, if we will steadfastly maintain that nothing is to be preferred to honor and that

---

[14] In Latin *virtus* (from *vir*) originally meant manliness or courage but came to mean all the virtues.

rem homini accidere posse, quae intolerabilis sit; quod facile ei persuadebitur, qui divinitatem et excellentiam humani animi noverit, quem turpe tantum atque inhonestum factum inficere potest: caetera vero, quae maxima putantur mala, dolores inquam, labores, tormenta, ac denique mors, si constanter ferantur ac fortiter, perficiunt, magisque egregium praestant.

Hic operaeprecium erit cogitatione versare plurima a maioribus nostris constantissime gesta, et cuiuscunque generis tormenta fortiter superata. Horum plerosque ante Christianam religionem, antiquitas est admirata; sed post effusam[7] Evangelii lucem tam magnam huiusmodi exemplorum copiam christiana [407] religio suppeditat, ut vix ulla cogitatione comprehendi queat.

Nullo pacto omittenda quoque erit magni excelsique animi virtus, cuius opera magnis etiam honoribus animus superior sit: unde appellationem sumpsit, dictaque est magnanimitas. Hanc Philosophi perfectionem irascibilis animae posuerunt, quia circa arduum quoddam versari videretur, quod proprie ad irascendi vim pertinet. eam vero, quae in mediocribus quibusdam est honoribus, in concupiscente, seu desiderativa animae parte statuerunt: quoniam nihil arduum propositum haberet. Hisce virtutibus, tanquam ad fortitudinem pertinentibus, firmatur animus, ne ab honore pendeat ex errore vulgi plerunque praestito, in quod vitium animi praestantes et egregiae naturae saepe numero incidere solent, nisi exculti prius fuerint tum recta quadam exististimatione, tum etiam magnanimitate. Nam cum honor virtutis sit praemium, virtutemque sequatur velut umbra corpus, prestans excellensque ingenium, si parumper ab honesto, quod virtutis est finis,

---

[7] Both V 14r and O 10r have "promulgatam" instead of "effusam."

nothing can happen to a person which is beyond endurance.[15] He will be easily persuaded of this who shall have known the divinity and excellence of the human soul, which can be tainted only by some shameful and dishonorable deed. The rest of those things which are considered supreme evils—sufferings, I say, labors, torments and finally death—perfect and make [one] more outstanding if they are borne with steadfast courage.

Here it will be worthwhile to ruminate over the many deeds our ancestors performed with great steadfastness and the torments of every sort that they overcame courageously. Before the Christian religion antiquity admired many of these men, but after the light of the Gospel was spread, the Christian religion supplies such a great abundance of examples of this sort that they almost surpass all comprehension.

Also the virtue of a great and lofty soul is by no means to be omitted; by its exertion the soul rises above even great honors: whence it takes its name and is called magnanimity. The philosophers posited this as a perfection of the irascible soul because it seemed to deal with something arduous, which properly pertains to the irascible power.[16] They place that power which involves certain minor honors in the concupiscible or desiderative part of the soul, because it does not have set before it anything arduous. These virtues, as they pertain to courage, strengthen the soul lest it depend upon an honor proffered often enough by a common error, a vice into which distinguished souls and outstanding natures again and again are prone to fall unless they shall have been previously educated both in certain right thinking and also in magnanimity. For since honor is the reward of virtue and follows virtue just as a shadow [follows] a body, a distinguished and excellent talent, if it shall have swerved aside for a short time from the honorable, which is the end of virtue, immedi-

---

[15] Confer Aquinas, S.T., II-II, 123, 3.

[16] Contarini's *magnanimitas* is the verbal equivalent for Aristotle's *megalopsychia*, which might be better translated as self-esteem. Contarini's discussion suggests that he may have had the *Eudemian Ethics* (III, 4-5) and the *Nicomachean Ethics* (IV, 3) in mind. Still, in making magnanimity a virtue of the soul's irascible part and subordinate to courage, which Aristotle does not do, Contarini comes closer to Stoic teaching. According to the anthologist Stobaeus, *Stoicorum Veterum Fragmenta*, edited by Johann von Arnim (Stuttgart: Teubner, 1903-24) III, 264, the Stoics "hold that some virtues are primary, others subordinate to the primary. The primary virtues are four: prudence, temperance, courage, justice .... To courage are subordinate endurance, confidence, magnanimity, cheerfulness, industriousness ...."

deflexerit, continuo pro virtutis fine honorem sibi proponit, quam actionum omnium postremum finem: id putant excelsi, atque magni viri esse, ut vitam etiam pro laude paciscantur, hanc vero laudem, atque gloriam (qui maximus est error) iudicio vulgi metiuntur: inde fiunt saepe ambitiosi, et addicti penitus aurae populari. quamobrem cum locus hic tam lubricus sit praestantibus egregiisque naturis, maxime cavendum erit, illi presertim, qui aliis regendis idoneum se esse profiteatur, et velit, ne quandoque corruat in pernitiosam hanc ambitionis voraginem. omni ergo conatu formandus ipsi animus erit hac fortitudinis specie, magnanimitate scilicet, praestabitque se magnis honoribus dignum, qui si pro meritis ipsi a vulgo non deferantur, negliget ac parvipendet; unde fit, ut difficillimum sit magnanimum esse, quia valde arduum quoque est magnis honoribus esse dignum; ex quibus efficitur, ut valde ridiculus, ac vanus sit habendus ille, qui, cum honoribus sit indignus, se magnanimum hisce contemnendis esse profiteri audeat.

Sequitur magnificentia, quae circa magnos est sumptus (hoc namque et ipsum arduum est) quam nolim a Christiani gregis praeside in hanc partem usurpari, ut ad animi hanc, quam statuo, magnificentiam attinere arbitretur, magnos coenarum, ac splendidos apparatus, ingentem famulorum ordinem, magnam et eximiam aulaeorum ac vasorum argenteorum supellectilem, caeterasque huiusmodi impensas, ut turpiores nunc omittam. non enim eadem quamcunque personam decent. in principe fortasse non indecora haec erunt, et magnificentiam spectabunt; at Episcopo, Christianique gregis pastori, nihil (ut existimo) magis indecens. verum magnificentiae Episcopi interesse reor, primum ut erga inopes profusissimus sit, magnaque hospitia construat, in quibus pauperum praesertim cum aegrotant, et victui et sanitati consulatur: deinde ut templa, vasa, vestes, caeteraque quae ad divinum cultum pertinent, quantum fieri possit, non omisso interim erga pauperes officio, magnifica ornataque habeat. ab hisce rebus Episcopo debetur magnificentiae laus.

ately proposes honor to itself as the ultimate end of all its actions instead of as the end of virtue. They regard it characteristic of noble and great men that they trade away even their life for praise; indeed they measure this praise and glory (this is the greatest mistake) on the basis of popular opinion, whence they often grow ambitious and wholly given over to popularity seeking. Wherefore since this place is so slippery for distinguished and outstanding natures, the person who declares himself to be suited to rule others and wishes to do so, must especially use extreme caution lest he sometime fall into this deadly whirlpool of ambition. Therefore by every effort he will have to develop for himself a soul with this type of courage, namely magnanimity, and he will make himself worthy of great honors who ignores and counts it for little if [honors] are not conferred on him by the crowd in accord with his deserts. Thus it happens that it is very difficult to be magnanimous because it is also very hard to be worthy of great honors.[17] Hence it happens that he is to be accounted very silly and empty-headed who, when he is unworthy of honors, dares to proclaim himself magnanimous in his spurning of these [honors].

Magnificence comes next. This concerns great outlays (this too is itself hard).[18] I would not want the ruler of the Christian flock to make use of it in such a way that he should think that this magnificence of the soul, which I am proposing, pertains to great and glittering table service for banquets, a vast row of servants, large and exceptional collection of tapestries and silver vases, and the other expenses of this sort, if I may now omit more shameful things. These things are not fitting for anybody. Perhaps they will not be out of place for a prince, and they will relate to magnificence. But nothing (in my view) is more unsuitable for a bishop and pastor of the Christian flock. Rather I think the magnificence of a bishop relates first to his being very generous toward the needy and his building great hospices in which provision is made for the feeding and health of the poor, especially when they are sick. Secondly, as far as possible he should have splendid and elegant churches, chalices, vestments and the other things that relate to divine worship, without meanwhile neglecting his duty to the poor. A bishop deserves praise for his magnificence in these things.

---

[17] Confer Aquinas, S.T., II-II, 129, 1.
[18] Confer Aquinas, S.T., II-II, 134, 3.

Reliqua ex virtutibus irascibilis appetitus est mansuetudo, qua mollitur animus, ac refraenatur, ne iracundiae stimulis in [408] praeceps actus rationem revocantem nequaquam audiat, sed longissime praecurrat. nam quemadmodum tribus superioribus virtutibus praestatur quoddam animo robur, ne rebus arduis cedat, neve praecurrentem rationem deserat: ita contra mansuetudine fraenatur irascendi vis, ne rationem praecurrat, eiusque mandatis obaudiat. Haec virtus maxime splendet in quovis praeside, furere enim valde alienum existimari debet a principe, in quo omnium maxime sapientiam optare solemus. nulla vero animi perturbatio magis homines agit in furorem, quam iracundia, ex qua non tantum in animo, verumetiam in corpore magna turbatio excitatur. licet intueri ora, gressus, omnemque habitum corporis hominis irati: nihil decorum; nihil compositum spectabis. Hae fere virtutes sunt a Peripateticis connumeratae, quibus sensibilis appetitus, qui suapte natura rationis est expers, neque ullum honesti sensum habet, quodammodo ad participationem rationis assurgit.

Nunc tempus poscere videtur, ut pauca quaedam, quae ad hoc negotium pertinent, dicamus de virtutibus partis rationalis. Nam ex hac, veluti ex radice quadam, rectitudo influit in reliquas quoque animi vires. Nisi enim haec recte in sua actione versabitur, frustra reliquae vires sequentur imperium rationis: at recte agere non poterit, nisi propriis virtutibus fuerit prius imbuta: huius autem animi vis

Gentleness is the last of the virtues belonging to the irascible appetite. It soothes and reins in the soul lest reacting headlong to the spurs of irascibility it does not listen to reason, which calls it back, but rushes far ahead. For just as the three previous virtues provided a certain strength to the soul lest it yield in harsh circumstances or desert reason which is racing ahead, so on the other hand gentleness reins in the irascible power so that it does not outrun reason but obeys its commands. This virtue shines splendidly in any ruler, for to rage with anger ought to be considered to be completely foreign to a prince, in whom we are wont to hope for wisdom above all else. No turmoil of soul more throws men into fury than does anger, by which a great turbulence of not only the soul but also the body is stirred up. One may look at the face, the stride, the whole arrangement of the body of an angry man: you will see nothing proper, nothing composed. The Peripatetics enumerate roughly these as the virtues by which the sensible appetite, which of itself by its nature is devoid of reason and has no sense of the honorable, somehow rises up to a participation in reason.[19]

The time now seems to demand that we say a few things which relate to this business about the virtues of the rational part [of the soul]. For from this, as from a sort of root, rectitude flows in to the other powers of the soul as well. For unless this will be rightly engaged in its action, the other powers would follow the command of reason in vain. But it will be unable to act rightly unless it will earlier have been steeped in its proper virtues. One power of this soul un-

---

[19] Aristotle discusses the moral virtues in Books III-V of his *Nicomachean Ethics*; he also lists the moral virtues in his *Eudemian Ethics*, II, 3. Aristotle's discussion includes courage, temperance, liberality, magnificence, pride or self-esteem, sense of shame or modesty, justice and equality, plus several other qualities for which he does not supply a proper name: ambition or love of honor, good temper or gentleness, friendliness, truthfulness, and tactfulness or modesty. Contarini's discussion of the virtues is somewhat different and includes the following: *temperantia, liberalitas, affabilitas, urbanitas, simplicitas, fortitudo, magnanimitas, magnificentia, mansuetudo, justitia.* Contarini comes closer to Aquinas (S.T., II-II), who devotes questions to temperance (Q. 141), liberality (Q. 117), affability (Q. 114), fortitude (Q. 123), magnanimity (Q. 129), magnificence (Q. 139), gentleness (Q. 157) and justice (Q. 58). The two virtues added by Contarini (*urbanitas, simplicitas*) seem qualities cherished by Contarini and many Venetian noblemen. On the other hand, Contarini depends on Aristotle for his discussion of the parts or powers of the soul: *De anima* III, 3ff. (432a 15ff.); *Nicomachean Ethics* I, 13 (1220a 13); and *Eudemian Ethics* II, 1 (1219b 27-1220a 13). I am indebted to William Dooley for providing me with most of these sources.

altera comprehendit, raciocinatur ac cogitat; altera vero appetitus quidam est cogitationis assecla. huius posterioris, appetitus inquam, rationalis iustitia perfectio est. non enim in sensibili appetitu recte haec animi virtus potuit collocari: nam non versatur circa sedandas perturbationes ut reliquae, sed tantum aequum ac servat ac tenet. aequum vero collatione discursuque rationis comprehenditur, et iccirco ad sensibilem partem pertinere non potuit, sed ad rationalem. huius namque multorum invicem collatio propria quaedam est actio. iccirco in eo appetitu, qui rationem sequitur, iustitiam collocarunt. Haec vero virtus, si in genere sumatur, tam late patet, ut ad eam caeterarum omnium virtutum actiones referri quaeant. quodsi pressius eam sumpseris, aequitatem tantum amplectitur in externis bonis, ut non plus sibi, quam aequum sit, neque alteri minus, sed aequum omnibus tribuatur. hominum quidem communitati, coetuique civili tam necessaria est haec animi virtus, ut ausim dicere sine reliquis virtutibus consistere posse hominum societatem, at numquam ne vel temporis momentum permansuram, si quaevis iustitia auferatur. in privato viro satis iustitiae esse putandum est, si ab inferenda iniuria abstinet, at in principe ac praeside late patet. Nam non satis est principi, si inferenda iniuria temperet ipse, verum oportet, ut et illatam ab alio iniuriam poena compenset, et ne inferatur pro virili provideat. qua in re tum mira prudentia, tum etiam diligentia non mediocri opus erit. Hanc igitur principum ac praesidum propriam peculiaremque virtutem, futurum Episcopum admirari oportet, a tenerisque annis assuescere, ut non modo facere, sed ne audire quidem iniustum aliquid patiatur. Hanc et in commutationibus servari curabit, et in distributionibus, quod praesidis officium est, diligentissime servabit.

Altera virtutum rationalis animi in ea est parte constituta, quae ratiocinatur et sapit. Hanc [409] prudentiam nominabimus latiori quadam significatione, quam a Peripateticis sumatur. Haec virtutum omnium princeps, sine qua nullum virtutis officium rectum esse

derstands, considers and thinks, another [power] is a sort of appetite, a servant of thought. Justice, I say, is the perfection of this second rational appetite. This virtue of the soul could not be rightly located in the sensible appetite, for it is not engaged in calming disorders like the other [virtues] but only preserves and upholds fairness. Fairness is understood by means of a comparison and consideration done by reason and therefore could not pertain to the sensible part [of the soul] but to the rational [part]. Comparing many things is in turn a certain specific action of this [rational part]. Hence they locate justice in that appetite which follows reason. Indeed, this virtue, if it is understood in general, has so wide a scope that the actions of all the other virtues can be referred to it. But if you understand it more narrowly, it only embraces fairness in external goods so that more is not allotted to oneself than is fair, nor less to another but a fair share to all. This virtue of the soul is so necessary to the human community and civil society that I would dare to say that human society can manage without the other virtues but it would never last even a moment of time if every sort of justice were taken away. Enough justice should be thought to exist in a private individual if he refrains from inflicting injury, but it has a wider scope in a prince and ruler. For it is not enough for a prince that he himself refrain from inflicting injury, but he ought to compensate by punishment for an injury inflicted by another and take care with all his strength that it not be inflicted. In this matter he will need both marvelous prudence and also no ordinary diligence. The future bishop needs to admire this specific and peculiar virtue of princes and rulers and needs to grow accustomed from his tender years to keep himself not only from acting unjustly but he should even refuse to listen to any injustice. He will take care that it is observed in business dealings, and he will guard it most diligently in distributions because that is a ruler's duty.

Another of the virtues of the rational soul is situated in that part which reasons and evaluates.[20] We will call this prudence with a certain broader meaning than the Peripatetics employ.[21] This is the prince of all the virtues, without which no right performance of vir-

[20] Confer Aquinas, S.T. II-II, 47, 1.

[21] Aristotle, who treats prudence in the *Nicomachean Ethics* VI, 5 (1140a 24ff.), gives a more limited role to prudence than that of Contarini's *virtutum omnium princeps*. The role Contarini assigns to prudence ("to look into what is fitting and honorable in each and every action") is assigned to wisdom by Aristotle.

potest. huius proprium est, quod in una quaque actione decorum, atque honestum sit intueri. quae licet quodam modo non in cive libero solum qui tum sui, tum familiae curam habet, sed etiam in servo esse debeat: hic tamen angustis quibusdam terminis coercetur, in principe vero ac praeside, quibus alii obediunt, proprios ac latissimos fines habet. non enim huic satis erit compertum habuisse, quid certo cuidam hominum generi in civitate et decens, et utile sit, sed in universis generibus, ut hoc norit, oportet. huius praecipua pars, quae omnium maxime principi convenit, est legum ferendarum facultas, ut scilicet leges ferat, quarum observantia cives civilem foelicitatem mancam illam, quam diximus, adipiscantur; Habiles autem atque apti fiant ad christianas virtutes capessendas, quarum demum ope supremam beatitudinem consequantur. at enim prudentiam meo quidem iudicio difficile adipiscetur, qui philosophiae morali nullam operam dederit; quo fit ut ea studia pulcherrima et Principe maxime digna existimem. in his vellem ego Episcopum nostrum, quem instituimus, dies atque noctes versari. Historiarum quoque cognito non parum ad prudentiam facit, dum aliorum exemplis illustrium alioqui virorum, quid deceat, et quid operaeprecium sit in una quaquae actione facile discimus. Huic quoque virtuti copulemus reliquarum rerum cognitionem, prae omnibus vero naturalium, divinarumque rerum contemplationem: quae et per se pulcherrima est, maximeque momentum praebet, ut ad earum rerum imitationem, atque exemplum, tum animi eorum, qui illam perceperint, tum universa civitas illorum ductu se effingat.[8] prudentiae quoque officium est, ut novas quasdam, superstitiosasque artes a veris honestisque dignoscat, ne fortasse (qui multorum est error) in monstris quibusdam, et nugis magno cum dispendio tempus terat.

Hactenus eas virtutes persecuti sumus, quibus humana vita continetur, ut prius illud in Episcopo nostro caveretur, ne quandoque ex homine in brutum animal degeneraret. Nam cum Episcopus (ut supra diximus) hominem quodam modo excedat, nostrumque institutum fuerit, de integro Episcopum ab incunabilis constituere, necesse fuit, ut prius hominem faceremus; quem postmodum Episcopum facturi essemus. Hucusque procedunt humanae vires,

---

[8] Here V 18v and O 12v have "atque exemplum tum animi nostri vires, tum universam civitatem effingat."

tue can exist. Its specific task is to look into what is fitting and honorable in each and every action. Although it is rightful somehow not only for a free citizen who has to take care of both himself and his family, it ought also be found in a slave. Here, however, it is restricted to certain narrow limits; in a prince and ruler, whom others obey, it has its proper and very ample boundaries. For him it is not enough to have worked out what is fitting and useful for a certain class of persons in the city, but he ought to get to know this for all the classes. The main part of this, which of all things is most appropriate for a prince, is skill in establishing laws, namely that he establish laws by whose observance the citizens may attain to that incomplete civic happiness of which we spoke. Let them be apt and suited for eagerly acquiring Christian virtues, by whose help they in the end attain to supreme beatitude. But in my judgment the person who shall have made no effort at moral philosophy will gain prudence only with difficulty. Thus it happens that I rate those studies the most beautiful and most worthy of a prince. I would like our bishop, whom we are training, to be engaged in these [studies] day and night. Moreover, a knowledge of history helps no little bit toward prudence since we easily learn, by the example of other men distinguished in other ways, what is fitting and what is worthwhile in any given action. We also link the knowledge of other things with this virtue, above all the contemplation of natural and divine things. This is most beautiful in itself and provides a mighty impetus so that both the souls of those who understand it and also the whole city reshape themselves by their leadership through the imitation and example of these [natural and divine] things. It is also the task of prudence to distinguish certain new and superstitious arts from the true and honorable lest perhaps (which is the mistake of many) time be wasted at great expense on portents and foolishness of some sort.

So far we have traced those virtues by which human life is held together so that our bishop might have some advanced warning lest at some point he might degenerate from being a man into being a brute animal. For as we said above, since a bishop in a certain way goes beyond being a man, our training will have aimed at molding a bishop completely from the crib, it was necessary that we should first construct the man, whom afterwards we would make into a bishop. Human powers go only this far and do not take a

neque ultra hominem promovent, quam ut in *nationibus* {actionibus} quibuscunque decorum, honestumque servet, ac divina quoquo pacto attingat ex rerum sensibilium contemplatione, admirabilique in rebus omnibus naturae ordine. Haec manca illa, atque imperfecta foelicitas est, ad quam supra dixi posse hominem naturali lumine pervenire. Verum non est haec suprema illa beatitudo: quae omni ex parte appetitum hominis compleat. sed quaerenda est multo excellentior, ad quam consequendam nunquam sufficerent naturales conatus, sed opus homini est peculiari quadam gratia divinitus impertita, nonnullisque virtutibus consequentibus gratiam, quarum adiumento humanus animus ad quandam participationem divinae naturae attollitur: hae vero sunt veluti [410] elementa supremae illius foelicitatis, quae sola animum implere potest, nihil enim aliud est summa hominis beatitudo, quam Deum fieri adeptione divinitatis, eoque bono foelicem esse, quo semper Deus est foelix. Hoc summum supremumque bonum sola christiana religio praestare potest, in qua per fidem legemque[9] Iesu Christi Dei et hominis ad assequendam divinitatem pervenire speramus; in quo certe tanquam in arctissimo[10], indissolubilique nexu queunt tam longe distantes naturae divina inquam, atque humana coniungi. nam cum divina congruit, quia personam Dei gerit. nec ab homine discrepat, cum sit homo; quo fit, ut in ipso possit homo Deum comprehendere (ut ita dicam) divinasque actiones imitari. Hoc illud est Dei arcanum et reconditum[11] mysterium, quod stulti philosophi non intelligentes interdum christianam religionem derident.

sed revertatur oratio, unde degressa est. Excellentissimus hic finis, quem consequi expetit christiana religio, perfecte in hoc mortali vita obtineri non potest. sed satis homini esse debet, si dum in vivis agit, semina quaedam[12] consequatur, ad eum finem adipiscendum. id namque in quibuscunque naturae effectibus clarissime conspicitur, si non statim debitam sibi attigerint perfectionem, priusquam absolutam obstineant, obtinere inchoatam. quamobrem oportuit hominis animum christianis ac divinis virtutibus supra se quodam modo attolli, paulatimque ad divina progredi, ut sic affectus post obitum absolute perfecteque beatitudinem consequeretur. Hi

---

[9] The word *legemque* is not found in either V 19v or O 13r.
[10] Both V 19v and O 13r read "aptissimo."
[11] Neither V 19v nor O 13v have "et reconditum."
[12] Both V 19v and O 13v have "semina quaedam et principia."

man further than achieving what is fair and honorable in any *na-tions* {actions} and that one somehow attains to divine things from the contemplation of sensible objects and from the admirable order to be found in all things. This is that incomplete and imperfect happiness to which I said earlier a man can attain by his natural light. But this is not that supreme beatitude which fulfills man's appetites in every respect. Rather a far more excellent one is to be sought; to attain it, natural efforts would never suffice; rather man has need for a certain special grace divinely imparted and for certain virtues consequent on grace, by whose help the human soul is lifted up to a certain participation in the divine nature. These are indeed like elements of that supreme happiness, which alone can fill the soul, for the highest beatitude of man is none other than that he should become God by obtaining divinity and should be happy by that good by which God is forever happy. This highest and supreme good is offered only by the Christian religion, wherein through the faith and law of Jesus Christ, God and man, we hope to arrive at the divinity we are seeking. Certainly in him natures, which are so far distant, the divine, I say, and the human, are able to be joined together as if in a most tight and indissoluble bond. For he comes together with the divine [nature] because he bears the person of God. Nor is he discordant from man since he is a man. Thus it happens that in him man is able to encompass God (if I may speak this way) and imitate divine actions. This is that secret and hidden mystery of God because of which foolish philosophers, in their failure to understand, sometimes mock the Christian religion.[22]

But let my discourse return to the point from which it digressed. This most excellent end, to which the Christian religion strives to attain, cannot be perfectly obtained in this mortal life. But it ought to be enough for man if, while he is yet among the living, he gains certain seeds for obtaining that end. For it is clearly seen in all of nature's effects that if they do not reach their proper perfection immediately, they do obtain an inchoative [perfection] prior to an absolute one. Wherefore the human soul ought to have been uplifted somehow above itself by Christian and divine virtues and gradually to progress to divine things so that thus developed it may after death absolutely and perfectly attain beatitude. These

[22] Here Contarini echoes 1 Cor 1:21-22 and 2:7-8.

christiani animi habitus facultatem intellectus nostri excedunt: quod maxime congrue modoque in primis naturali contingit. evehunt namque hominis animum ad eam perfectionem, a qua homo longissime distat, idem licet intueri in habitibus sensibilis appetitus de quibus quam plurima a nobis sunt superius explicata. illi[13] quoque sensitivam vim ad honestum appetendum, quod nequaquam suapte natura sensibilis anima appetit, verum convenit superiori virtuti, rationi (inquam), mirum ergo nulli esse debet, si christianis, quibus proposita est divini boni adeptio, quaedam sunt propriae peculiaresque virtutes, quas philosophi, qui tantum naturae lumine aguntur, nunquam perspicere potuerunt.

his igitur christianis seu divinis virtutibus, maxime non dicam imbutus, sed ornatus, et excultus esse debet is, quem instituimus, Episcopus; adeo ut ex sua plenitudine commissam sibi impleat civitatem. tres huiusmodi virtutes Theologi numerant, quarum una, fides scilicet, pertinet ad intellectum, duae vero, spes inquam et charitas, ad voluntatem. harum prima est fides. absolutissima vero est charitas, sine qua nihil *possunt* {prosunt} quaecunque aliae virtutes. fides quarundam rerum divinarum cognitionem nobis praestat; ad quas capessendas intellectus sibi ipse non est satis. Haec omnia ea sunt, quae in sacris litteris continentur, ac certa ratione potest cuilibet compertum esse, oportuisse in huiusmodi quibusdam intellectum hominis exerceri, ut fieret divinitatis capax. Hoc namque praecipue observandum his, qui in cognitione divinorum proficere cupiunt, tum penitus videlicet ab homine ignorari Deum cum putatur aliqua ex parte comprehendi, quid sit. quapropter Dionysius Areopagita summus divinorum scrutator, Dei cognitionem [411] summam appellat scientiam divinae ignorationis. ut ergo hoc homini penitus insideret, Dei naturam

---

[13] V 20r and O 13v have "Evehunt illi" etc.

Christian habits of the soul surpass the faculty of our intellect—something that happens very appropriately and in a very natural way. For they carry the human soul to that perfection which is extremely distant from man; the same can be seen in the habits of the sensible appetite about which we spoke at some length above. They [the Christian virtues] also [exceed] the sensitive power for seeking the honorable, which the sensible soul never seeks of its own nature. Rather this belongs to a higher power, to reason, I say. Hence it should surprise no one if Christians, for whom there has been proposed the acquisition of divine goodness, have certain proper virtues of their own which the philosophers, who were working only by the light of nature, could never perceive.

The bishop whom we are educating therefore should be (I will not go to the length of saying steeped in) equipped and ennobled by these Christian or divine virtues—even to the degree that from his fullness he may enrich the city entrusted to him. The theologians enumerate three virtues of this sort, of which one, namely faith, pertains to the intellect and two, hope and charity, I say, to the will. The first of these is faith. The most perfect is charity, without which all the other virtues *can do* {can be of value for} nothing. Faith furnishes us with knowledge of certain divine things which are beyond the power of the intellect by itself to grasp. These are all the things which are contained in the holy scriptures; and anybody can discover by certain argument that the intellect of man ought to be practiced in some things of this sort so that he might become capable of the divinity. This especially must be noted by those who desire to make progress in the knowledge of divine things, namely that man is utterly ignorant of God at the point when one thinks he grasps in some part what [God] is. Hence Dionysius the Areopagite, the best investigator of things divine, calls the highest knowledge of God the science of divine ignorance.[23] So that the fact of God's nature being

[23] Contrary to Lorenzo Valla and Erasmus but in agreement with many of his contemporaries, Contarini seems to accept as genuine works of St. Paul's convert Dionysius the Areopagite (Acts 17:34) the body of writings which circulated under his name but were in fact written around 500 A.D. by an unknown author, now usually referred to as Pseudo-Dionysius, who was enormously influential. He returns repeatedly to apophatic theology—that God utterly surpasses our ability to understand or describe him; good examples are found in Colm Luibheid, translator, *Pseudo-Dionysius: The Complete Works* (New York: Paulist Press, 1987) 109 (*The Divine Names*, 872A) and 138-41 (*The Mystical Theology*, 1032A-1048B).

longissime distare ab omni eo, quod intellectus noster cogitat, necesse fuit quaedam de Deo credenda his proponi, quae omnino mentis aciem superarent; quibus tanquam finis proposita est nuda, apertaque divinae naturae contemplatio. fidem spes sequitur. fieri namque non posset, ut quispiam bono illius potiundo accingeretur, quod nequaquam speraret adipisci. Haec virtus fortitudini quodam modo respondet, nam animum firmat, ut ne difficultate rei, ac prope desperatione terreatur. quare si rationali appetitui adhiberi posset ea differentia, quam sensitivo adhibuimus, ut scilicet divideretur in vim desiderandi ac irascendi; perfectionem irascibilis rationalis, spem utique statueremus.

Omnibus hisce virtutibus tam moralibus, quam divinis supremam manum imponit charitas, absolutionemque praestat. Hac virtute tam egregie assurgit animus hominis, ut iam non in se ipso, sed in Deo vivere incipiat. nam cum caetera omnia, tum etiam seipsum in Deo amat vir perfectus charitate. huius vi morales virtutes attolluntur ad altiorem, sublimioremque finem, vel, ut nonnulli perhibent, novae quaedam in animum influunt excellentes, atque egregiae magis, quam morales. honestum namque et decorum, qui prastitutus finis erat virtuti morali, a bono divino longissime abest; quo tanquam fine omnium virtutum, actiones moderatur charitas. hoc in loco non absurde puto dicemus, si actioni honestae, ac propterea decorae dixerimus vitam quandam praestari a charitate; sine qua honestum, quod philosophi tanti faciunt, friget quodam modo ac marcescit. huius rei similitudinem ipse fingere potes, si unquam pulcherrimi alicuius cadaver, seu marmoream statuam a Praxitele summo artifice

enormously far from all that our intellect thinks might fully penetrate humans, it was necessary to propose to them some things they must believe about God that completely surpassed the mind's keenness. To them was proposed the naked and uncovered contemplation of the divine nature as their end.

Hope comes after faith. For it would be impossible for anybody to gird himself to gaining the good of that which he had no hope of acquiring. This virtue in a certain way corresponds to fortitude, for it strengthens the soul lest it be frightened away by the difficult nature of the thing and by near despair. Hence if that distinction could be applied to the rational appetite that we applied to the sensitive, namely that it was divided into the desiderative and irascible powers, we would posit hope as the perfection of the irascible rational [appetite].[24]

Charity has the supreme role and confers perfection on all these virtues, both moral and divine. By this virtue the human soul rises up so exceptionally that it then begins to live not in itself but in God. The man made perfect in charity loves both all other things and also himself in God. By its power the moral virtues are lifted up to a higher, more sublime end, or as some suggest, certain new [virtues], excellent and more outstanding than the moral [virtues], flow into the soul.[25] For the honorable and fitting, which was the end assigned to moral virtue, is very distant from the divine good, by which, as the end of all the virtues, charity governs all actions. I do not think it absurd to claim at this point, that if we shall have said that charity grants a certain life to honorable and therefore fitting conduct, the honorable about which the philosophers boast so much, somehow freezes and fades without it. You yourself could fashion an analogy of this reality if you ever saw the body of some beautiful person or a marble statue most artfully sculpted by Praxiteles,[26] the supreme art-

---

[24] Here Contarini is in general agreement with Aquinas, who writes (S.T., II-II, 18, 1), "Therefore hope resides in the higher appetite, called the will, and not in the lower appetite, of which the irascible is a part." But in assigning an irascible part to the will (which Contarini does only conditionally: "si... adhiberi posset"), he goes beyond Aquinas and contradicts Aristotle, for whom the irascible part of the soul, regulated by courage, is intrinsically irrational and participates in reason only insofar as it obeys the promptings of the rational part.

[25] Confer Aquinas, S.T., I-II, 62.

[26] Praxiteles worked at Athens in the fourth century B.C. and was generally considered the greatest sculptor of his era.

diligentissime confectam vidisti: spectabis enim in utroque miram quandam membrorum formationem, atque egregiam harmoniam, ut nulla in parte suspicari queas praetermissum esse decorum. attamen pulchra ea statua iacet ac friget, cur? nempe, quia anima vitaque caret. pari ratione, honesta decoraque actio pulchra est, omni sibi ex parte respondet, considerantem oblectat: friget tamen, nisi a charitate vitam fuerit assecuta. Divinae igitur hae virtutes esse debent in Episcopo adeo excellentes, ut ab ipso in universam civitatem emanent, tanquam a quodam fonte perenni. primum namque oportet non ea solum credere, et nosse virum Episcopum, quae christianus quivis vel mediocriter in religione eruditus novit: verum etiam Theologiam christianam callere, ut alios docere queat christianum scilicet dogma, rationesque reddere occultarum rerum, ministerorumque[14] christianorum, et impugnantes refellere, tum ea quae iuris pontificii sunt probe nosse. in primis autem utrumque testamentum sic tenere,[15] ut ungues, digitosque suos, atque in ea lectione oblectare assidueque versari; ac postremo quaecunque alia studia ad haec referre. quod nostris temporibus omnium maxime praestandum est, cum turpe sit sacerdoti, et Episcopo non si Virgilianum carmen, aut huiusmodi quippiam non intellexerit, sed si Evangelium nunquam totum perlegerit, ac divinae scripturae spiritum non hauserit: quidque de sanctissima trinitate, de [412] sacrosancta eucharistia, caeterisque Sacramentis ac religionis christianae mysteriis credendum explicite sit, non curaverit.[16] Quod si in christianis omnibus studium aliquod,

[14] Both V 22v and O 14v read "mysteriorumque."

[15] Here V 22v and O 14v have "demum autem utrumque testamentum seu instrumentum, ut elegantiores dicunt, ..." The person charged with preparing the Paris edition probably replaced *demum* with *in primis* lest it seem that Contarini was putting other kinds of religious knowledge ahead of Scripture. He probably dropped "seu instrumentum, ut elegantiores dicunt" lest it be read as praise of Erasmus's first edition of the Greek New Testament, which had fallen into disfavor during the Counter Reformation. These arguments are developed by Gigliola Fragnito in her *Gasparo Contarini*, 146-147, 167.

[16] The Paris edition recasts this sentence to bring it closer to Counter Reformation attitudes. V 22v-23r and O 15v read: "quod nostris temporibus omnium minime prestatur quibus turpe ducunt sacerdoti ac episcopo si vergilianum carmen aut huiusmodi quippiam non intellexerit evangelium vero neque unquam totum perlegisse parvi momenti putant. Quid de Trinitate, de eucharistia aut de incarnatione Christi sentiendum numquam fortasse audierunt. Tamen eruditi ac docti sacerdotes et esse et haberi volunt. Praeposterum certe morem, maximeque ab officio episcopi alienum. Qua in re prophani quoque meo iudicio culpa non carent. At in sacerdoti procul dubio piaculo simili haberi debent. Nec minus in Episcopo spei virtus...." Fragnito discusses the change, *Gasparo Contarini*, 167-168.

ist, for in both of them you will gaze upon a certain wondrous formation of the limbs and an outstanding harmony so that in no part are you able to suspect that comeliness has been missed. Still that beautiful statue lies there and is cold. Why? Surely because it lacks a soul and life. With equal reason honorable and fitting conduct is beautiful, all its parts fit it, it gives enjoyment to the viewer. Still it is immobile unless charity confers life on it.

Therefore these divine virtues ought to be so outstandingly present in a bishop that they flow out from him into the whole city as if from some perennial fountain. For first of all the man who is bishop ought to believe and know not only those things which any Christian even moderately learned in religion knows, but [he should] also know by experience Christian theology so that he can teach others Christian dogma and provide reasons for hidden things and for the Christian ministries and can refute objectors and have a sound knowledge of things which pertain to pontifical law. But he must especially possess both the Testaments like his own fingernails and fingers and delight in and assiduously keep busy in reading them. Finally he should channel all his other studies to them. In our times above all this should be most expected since it is shameful for a priest and bishop, not if they shall not have understood a poem of Virgil or anything of the sort, but if he shall not have read through the whole Gospel and shall not have drunken in the spirit of the divine scripture and if he shall not have been concerned with what must be explicitly believed about the most holy Trinity, about the most sacred Eucharist, and the other sacraments and mysteries of the Christian religion. But if some study and some knowledge of heavenly matters is necessary for every Chris-

coelestiumque rerum scientia aliqua necessaria est, quanto magis in sacerdote requiritur? verum in Episcopo spei virtus latius patet, quam in privato viro; non enim divinum bonum sibi assequi solum sperare debet, verum etiam posse, Dei numine favente, commissam suae fidei civitatem promovere ad illud bonum consequendum. sibi ipsi tamen deesse non debet, quin animum paret ad divinas illustrationes suscipiendas, omnemque diligentiam, atque operam praestet in suo grege gubernando. Perfectio autem et absolutio horum omnium est charitas, quae cum christiano cuique, tum praecipue necessaria est pastori christiani gregis. quae virtus, cum praestantissima sit, atque reliquis virtutibus omnibus vitam praebeat, latissime manat, nulloque fere termino cohibetur, sed ad omnes spectat: iccirco opus erit ne erga dispares pari munere fungamur, ut rectus ordo servetur in officiis charitatis, sine quo nulla huiusmodi virtutis actio constabit. primum ergo Episcopi munus est, ut Deum prae omnibus amet, nihilque conferendum arbitretur, cum divini honoris ac laudis tuitione, prae qua et vitam, et ipsam denique foelicitatem nihili faciat, et ad hoc tanquam ad postremum finem referat omnes suas actiones, summopere enim et decus, et dignitatem Dei Episcopum sustinere decet. Mirabitur fortasse aliquis, alienumque a natura rerum arbitrabitur hoc praeceptum esse; cum omnibus rebus insitum natura videatur, ut maxime ac prae omnibus ament se ipsas. caeterum diligentius, ac interius re perspecta cuilibet compertum esse poterit, nequaquam hoc esse a naturae legibus alienum. nam cum omnia praecipue appetant esse, prae omnibus etiam naturali desiderio cupiunt eius conservationem, et incolumitatem; in quo putant maxime eorum esse constare. quamobrem natura fit, ut nonnulla, quorum esse magis sit in alio quopiam, quam in ipsis, magis optent illius, quam sui ipsorum conservationem. In promptu sunt partes, quarum esse consistit in ipsa integritate totius, eaque ratione se vel certissimo periculo exponunt pro totius incolumitate tuenda. Nullus ergo mirari debet, si noverit divinum esse cuiusque alterius rei esse continere, et magis in ipso consistere, quam in rebus ipsis, si secundum naturam esse diximus, cuius ordinem egregie christiana religio imitatur, magis oportere Deum a nobis amari, quam nosmetipsos;

tian, how much more is this required in a priest! But in a bishop the virtue of hope opens out more widely than in a private person; for he should not only hope to attain the divine good for himself but also, by the favor of God's divine power, he should be able to motivate the city entrusted to him so that it acquires the same good. He, however, ought not to let himself slacken in preparing his soul to receive divine illuminations and in employing all diligence and effort in governing his flock.

The perfection and summit of all these things is charity, which is needed by every Christian and especially by the pastor of the Christian flock. This virtue, since it is the most outstanding and gives life to all the other virtues, flows out most widely; it is checked by almost no limit but looks to all people. Wherefore there will be need lest we perform a like function for unlike people, so that a right order may be preserved in our charitable duties. Without this [order] no activity of such a virtue will hold up. Therefore the first duty of the bishop is to love God above all things and to consider nothing else comparable with safeguarding the divine honor and praise; compared to that, he should account both his own life and finally his own happiness as nothing. To this he should direct all his action as to their final end. Perhaps somebody will wonder whether it is fitting for a bishop to uphold so utterly both the honor and dignity of God, and he will think that this commandment is foreign to the nature of things since nature seems to have inserted into all things that they love themselves most and above all else. But when the question is examined more carefully and deeply, anybody will be able to discover that this is not at all foreign to the laws of nature. Since all things mainly desire existence, above all they also long with a natural desire for the conservation and safety of him upon whom they think their existence mostly depends. Hence it happens in nature that some things, whose existence is more in some other thing than in themselves, prefer its conservation more than their own. The parts, whose existence consists in the very integrity of the whole, are ready for that reason to expose themselves even to certain danger to protect the whole from injury. If one knows that the divine being contains the being of all other things and that their being exists in Him more than in the things themselves, (if we spoke in terms of nature whose order the Christian religion splendidly imitates), no one should be surprised that we ought to love God more than ourselves. Each person should,

post Deum, quia unumquodquoque magis est in se, quam in alio quopiam, salutem ac foelicitatem unusquisque procurare debet. hoc vero ab Episcopo praestabitur, si innocentissime vixerit, animumque quacunque labe purgarit. postremo inserviendum est alienae infoelicitati, ac egentibus opem ferre par est. qua in re valde Episcopo est enitendum, ne huiusmodi officio desit. hoc nanque praecipuum munus eius est, et quod a pastoribus christiani populi requiri maxime solet.

Non possum hoc in loco non magnopere miserari nostrae tempestatis calamitatem, cum paucos admodum christiani populi moderatores comperias, qui degant in civitatibus fidei eorum commissis. Verum satis officio suo fecisse putant, si procuratori regendam [413] urbem tradiderint, ipsi vero redditibus potiantur. ac magni quidem cuiuspiam in Romana curia pompam comitantur, regnorumque tractant, ac bellorum negotia, de populo vero cui praesunt, an in christiana religione proficiat, an deficiat, ne nuntium quidem accipiunt, egenosque gregis sui omnino negligunt et ignorant. hoccine est Episcopum gerere? hoccine discipulos Christi imitari, praeceptaque Evangelica servare? probus ergo Episcopus operam dabit ne alteri tradat gregem suum curandum, sed quam brevissimo tempore ab ovili aberit, nisi aliqua ratione a Pontifice evocatus alicui officio inserviat, quod ad emolumentum christianae Reipublicae spectet. verum non hanc dari sibi occasionem optet, neque tale quid ambiat; sed aegre ac fere invitus huiusmodi onus suscipiat. quo expedito, non aliud procuret, sed quam citissime ad gregem redeat.

In populi vero (cui praeest) gubernatione aequum quoddam servabit, certumque tenebit ordinem (nam hac in re charitas cum iustitia proportionem habet). primum igitur sacerdotum ac cleri magnam habeat curam, his enim ministris utatur opus est in sacris administrandis, populoque curando. quare quamoptimos sacerdotes habere, ac in christianis rebus eruditos magni momenti instar habet ad populi gubernationem, hos ergo erudire ac bonos facere praecipue ad ipsos spectat. deinde bonos viros instruet et diliget.

after God, look out for his salvation and happiness, because each and every thing exists more in itself than in any other thing. The bishop will indeed accomplish this if he shall have lived in a very innocent way and shall have cleansed his soul from all stain. Lastly one must care for others' unhappiness, and it is right to bring help to the needy. Here the bishop must make a strenuous effort lest he fall short in this sort of duty. For this is his main task and is what is usually most looked for in the pastors of the Christian people.

At this point I cannot fail to bewail greatly the disaster of our times, when you can find very few leaders of the Christian people who dwell in the cities entrusted to their faithful care. They think that they are performing their duty well enough if they shall have handed over the city's management to a procurator, while they take over the income. To be sure, they accompany the train of some important person at the Roman curia, they are engaged in negotiations over kingdoms and wars; but about the people over whom they have charge, they do not even get a report on whether these are making progress in the Christian religion or falling short. They wholly neglect and are ignorant about the needy among their flock. Is this to play the role of bishop? Is this to imitate the disciples of Christ and keep the commandments of the Gospel? Therefore the good bishop will take care not to hand over to another the care of his flock, but he will be absent from the sheep fold for the shortest possible time, unless for some reason the Pontiff call him to serve in some office which looks to the betterment of the Christian commonwealth. But let him not wish that this occasion be given to him nor should he go looking for something of the sort; rather let him undertake burdens of this kind reluctantly and almost unwillingly. The task accomplished, let him not take charge of another but return to his flock as quickly as possible.

In governing the people (over whom he has charge) he will preserve a certain fairness and will keep to a certain order (for in this matter charity is commensurate with justice). First let him have a great care for the priests and clergy, for there is need that he use these ministers in administering the sacred [rites] and caring for the people. Having the best priests possible and ones learned in Christian concerns has great importance for governing the people; to them mainly belongs the task of teaching these [people] and making them good.

pravis tamen curandis maior opera impendi debet. non enim (ut inquit Christus) est opus medico bene valentibus, sed aegrotis. virgines Christo dicatae, ne vitam ullo libidinis, aut lasciviarum genere polluant, quantum fieri potest, cavebit. Egenos, praesertim aegrotos, aut nobiles, quibus egestas ignominiae habetur, fovebit opibus ac redditibus suis. in quo officio si caetera paria in utroque sint, praeferendum puto virum bonum iniquo. vivendi norma servata (ut reor) optime praestabit charitatis munera. Nam ea ratione extra se quodam modo positus alienam rem aget, quod charitati peculiare est. cupiebat Moyses pro salute Israelitici populi deleri ex libro viventium. Paulus optabat anathema pro *patribus* {fratribus}, qui loci quo pacto sint intelligendi, nunc omittimus.

in praesentia sit satis dixisse charitatem ecstasim facere, ita ut extra se diffluat qui fuerit praeditus hac virtute, potiusque in aliis, quam in se vivat. quod etiam Deo contigisse in rerum creatione Dionysius dicit. ex amore, nanque ecstasim passus in alias creaturas defluxit, ac eas ita condidit. nuncque in illis existens quasi extra se in aliis continet ac conservat. quare clarissime paret nullum animi vitium charitati magis contrarium esse invidentia ac malevolentia. invidus nanque tantum bonum suum vult, alienum nollet: de proximi autem amici malo gaudium concipit, de successu maerorem. at contra, charitas aliena procurat, sua negligit. nec tamen ignoro interdum ex charitate quoddam odii genus excitari, quo odimus iniquos, quatenus iniqui sunt, ac de eorum successibus dolemus: cupimus tamen ut boni fiant, sicque affecti optatis fruantur. hoc odium perfectum appellat David in psalmo, super inimicos tuos (inquit) tabescebam, perfecto odio oderam illos, et inimici facti sunt mihi: haec est ea virtus, quam indignationem Peripatetici nominant quam in medio

Secondly, let him teach and love good men. But he ought to expend greater effort in curing the vicious. For (as Christ says) it is not those in good health that need a doctor but those who are sick. As far as possible he will take care that virgins dedicated to Christ do not befoul their life with any lust or anything lascivious. He will favor with his help and his income the needy, especially the sick or the nobles, for whom poverty involves shame. As to this duty, if other things are equal on both sides, I think a good man is to be preferred to an evil one. The style of life one observes (as I think) will best provide the duties of charity. For this reason a man somehow is taken out of himself and deals with an outside task, which is peculiar to charity. Moses desired to be blotted from the book of the living for the salvation of the Israelite people.[27] Paul wanted to be anathema for *the fathers* {the brothers};[28] we omit for now how these passages should be understood.

For the present let it be enough to have said that charity brings on ecstacy so that the person who has been endowed with this virtue flows out beyond himself and lives in others rather than in himself. Dionysius says this also happened to God in the creation of things.[29] Out of love he underwent ecstacy and flowed into other creatures, and he thus created them. Now, existing in them as if out of himself in them, he embraces and conserves [them]. So it should appear very clearly that no vice of the soul is more opposed to charity than envy and malevolence. For the envious man wants only his own good and does not want the other's [good]: but he gets enjoyment from an evil that befalls a dear neighbor and sadness from his success. In contrast, charity looks after the interest of others [and] neglects its own. But I am not unaware that occasionally charity stirs up a certain hatred whereby we hate the wicked in so far as they are wicked, and we bewail their successes. Still we desire that they become good and that after being made so they may enjoy what they have desired. This is what David calls a perfect hatred in the psalm, "I loathe your enemies (he says), I hate them with a perfect hatred; they have become my own enemies."[30] This is that virtue which the Peripatetics call

---

[27] Exod 32:32.
[28] Rom 9:3.
[29] Luibheid edition, p. 115 (*The Divine Names*, 909C).
[30] Ps 139:21-22.

statuunt [414] malevolentiae, et invidentiae. Satis ut arbitror hucusque generali quadam forma Episcopum nostrum effinximus, dedimusque operam, ut prius hominem, deinde Episcopum formaremus. nunc quae supersunt, in alterum volumen differimus.

LIBER SECUNDUS

Multum diuque dubitatum est apud veteres rerum scrutatores, humanum ne genus religioni divinoque cultui natura duce inserviret, an potius consilio quodam, ac sapientum instituto, qui homines in officio contineri non posse arbitrati sunt, si Deorum metus ac reverentia de medio sublata esset. verum ipsam rem paulo attentius consideranti manifestissimum esse potest, hoc minime humanum fuisse commentum, sed ita natura comparatum esse, ut quemadmodum homines civilem vitam naturali quadam propensione agunt; nec non loquendi usum (quod nulli animantium generi contigit) a natura sortiti sunt, ita etiam naturalibus quibusdam stimulis homo actus ad divinum cultum contenderet. quod puto tum ratione, tum reipsa facillime comprobari. Cum enim cuiusque rei perfectio tunc penitus absolvatur, cum ad eam conversa fuerit causam, quam substantiae, atque esse habuerit auctorem; ut hac ratione veluti solidum quendam circulum faciat; hominis vero animus, quo praecipue eius substantia constat, Deum optimum habeat auctorem: nihil mirum videri debet, si naturali innataque inclinatione convertatur ad Deum, quem colat, ac veneretur.

huic rationi res ipsa firmam facit fidem. Nam neque ullis unquam temporibus gentem aliquam fuisse, neque hac tempestate inveniri, vel in extremis oceani littoribus, vel in insulis penitus a reliquo orbe divisis, memoriae proditum est; apud quem nullus esset Deorum cultus: licet de diis alia alii sentiant; maluntque bovi aut igni, aut faxeo vel aeneo simulacro divinum cultum praestare;

indignation; they situate it as the mean between malevolence and envy.[31] I think that so far we have sufficiently delineated our bishop in a certain general outline and have taken care that we formed first the man, then the bishop. Now we postpone to a second book the things that still remain.

BOOK TWO

There has long been considerable controversy among the ancients who studied events whether the human race was led by nature to be devoted to religion and divine worship or rather by some suggestion or arrangement by wise persons who thought that people could not be held to their duty if fear and reverence for the gods were removed from their midst.[32] But it can become very clear to somebody who examines the subject itself a bit more closely, that this is hardly a human contrivance but something which nature has fitted together just as men conduct their civil life by a certain natural inclination. Likewise they have been acquired by nature the use of speech (which has happened to no species of brute animal); so also man, moved by certain natural promptings, reaches out toward divine worship. I think this can be very easily proved by both reason and the experience itself since the perfection of anything is fully achieved at the moment when it has turned toward the cause which it has as author of its substance and existence: so that for this reason it makes something like a solid circle. The mind of man, in which his substance mainly consists, has the good God as its author. It should not seem in the least surprising if he is turned by a natural and innate inclination to God, so as to worship and honor Him.

Experience itself fortifies faith in this argument. It has never been recorded that any tribe in any age has existed among whom there was not some worship of the gods, nor at this time can one be found even on the farthest shores of the ocean or on islands totally remote from the rest of the globe. Admittedly different people held different views about the gods. They preferred to pay divine worship to bulls or fire or to flaming or bronze images than to be completely without any

---

[31] Aristotle, *Nicomachean Ethics*, II, 7 (1108b 1-6).
[32] Livy I, 19; Cicero, *De natura deorum*, I, i-ii; Ovid, *Ars amatoria*, I, 637.

quam omni prorsus religione carere. quamobrem nulli dubium relinqui posse existimo, religionem naturaliter homini insitam esse, sicut et civilis vita et loquendi vis. verum natura, quemadmodum neque civiles mores et leges, neque sermonem, quae in homine inchoaverat, perfecit, sic utique religionem perficere non potuit. qua in re naturae vis longius a perfectione atque absolutione abfuit, quam in civilibus moribus et orationis facultate. Homo nanque vi luminis [415] naturalis paulatim pro populorum ac regionum ingenio utrumque eorum complevit, ut ex monumentis philosophorum, et oratorum patere cuilibet potest.

At religionem veram nisi divina ope adiutus nullus unquam potuit invenire. consideranti vero penitusque discutienti quascunque religiones, quae aut nostris, aut priscis temporibus aliae fuerint a christiana pietate, perspicuum erit vix ullam esse, quae hominem contineat in munere atque officio hominis, nedum ad altiora, sublimioraque promovet. sola vero christiana religio non solum hoc praestat, ut ne homo brutis appetitionibus inserviat neglecto imperio rationis, sed etiam nova quadam vita hominem imbuit divinae vitae participe. iccirco instituta sunt in Ecclesia Sacramenta, quibus veluti sensibilibus quibusdam signis, quorum cognitio de sensu pendet, nobis indicaretur, quid ex christiana pietate invisibiliter in animo fieret. primumque institutum fuit baptismatis seu ablutionis Sacramentum, per quod non solum significatur, verum etiam efficitur, ut vetus homo deponatur, sordibusque peccatorum ablutis, novus ac coelestis regeneretur.[17] verum sicut post naturalem corporeamque generationem praestatur naturae homini incrementum ac robor; ita etiam divina gratia secundum hanc spiritualem generationem praestatur homini robur in christiana pietate, adversus quascunque vel hominum vel daemonum oppugnationes. huius rei signum est in chrismate. deinde quemadmodum nisi iugi alimento calor hominis foveretur, continuo ad corruptionem tenderet; pari modo ad

---

[17] This sentence seems to have been recast in the Paris edition to clarify church teaching. V 28rv and O 17v read: "primumque institutum fuit baptismatis seu ablutionis sacramentum, in quo significatur veterem hominem ablui, novumque ac coelestem generari ex fide Iesu Christi qui, ut inquit Apostolus, semel mortuuus est peccato, nunc autem vivit Deo."

religion.[33] Therefore I do not think that there can be any doubt left in anyone that religion is naturally inherent in man just as are civil life and the power of speech.[34] But nature was not able to perfect religion any more than it could perfect civil customs and laws nor the speech that it began in man. In this area the power of nature fell short of perfection and completion far more than in civil customs and the faculty of speech. For man by the force of natural light, depending on the genius of peoples and places, gradually perfects both of them, as is clear to anybody from the achievements of philosophers and orators.

True religion, however, nobody was ever able to discover unless helped by divine aid. It will be clear to anybody who reflects on or delves deeply into the various religions which in our times or in early times were different from Christian piety that scarcely any [of them] restricted man to the duty and task of man, much less urged him to higher and more lofty things. The Christian religion alone truly not only accomplishes this so that a man does not become enslaved to animal appetites, neglecting the commands of reason, but also saturates man with a certain new life which partakes of divine life. Hence sacraments have been established in the Church by which, like certain visible signs, the knowledge of which depends on sense, we are instructed about what is taking place invisibly in the soul through Christian piety. The sacrament of baptism or cleansing was instituted first, through which it is not only signified but also brought about that the old man be put aside and the new and heavenly man be born again after the stains of sins have been washed away. Just as growth and strength of nature are given to man after his natural corporeal birth, so also strength in Christian piety against all the attacks of either men or demons is given man by divine grace through this spiritual generation. This event is signified by anointing. Secondly, just as human health immediately tends to corrupt unless it is as-

[33] Gigliola Fragnito, *Gasparo Contarini*, 170n, discusses the various sources from which Contarini might have drawn his knowledge of peoples whom Europeans had recently encountered, particularly in the Americas; Pietro Martire d'Anghiera's *De orbe novo decades* (especially I, 3 and 9; II, 3 and 6; III, 1) seems Contarini's most likely source.

[34] Here Contarini's view contrasts sharply with that of Machiavelli, whose *Discorsi*, written at roughly the same time, argued that religion was politically inspired and praised Numa for inventing the Roman religion so that fear of the gods would keep the early Romans submissive and moral: I, ch. 11.

fomentum divini caloris institutum est sanctissimum[18] eucharistiae Sacramentum, quo virtutes omnes fotae, vivicaque Christi carne nutritae hominem semper ad potiora melioraque promovent. accidunt saepenumero aegritudines et molestae, et perniciosae corpori. eis[19] pharmaci ope continuo occurrendum est. sic in christiana vita frequenter contingit, ut delictorum labe omnis prorsus divina gratia extinguatur. huic pernitosae aegritudini poenitentiae Sacramentum tanquam praesentaneum remedium est institutum. Ac quem morem medici servant, ut reliquias morbi levi quodam medicamento expurgent: eundem imitatur christiana religio in spirituali vita hominis, ut extremam adhibeat unctionem in exitu mortalis vitae, tanquam in aegritudinum fine, quibus continuis donec vitam ducimus vexamur, atque affligimur.

Verum cum unusquisque christicola, ex quibus tanquam ex membris constat mysticum corpus Ecclesiae, cuius caput est Christus, simul non sit; sed aliis alii in vita succedant, oportuit matrimonii, coniugalisque lecti Sacramentum institui, quod ad sanctam natorum propagationem spectat. his omnibus veluti postremum accedit Sacramentum ecclesiasticorum ordinum, qui ad generationem spiritualem, vitamque ac robur, nec non pharmaca ea praestanda, de quibus supra meminimus, sunt divinitus instituti. ut, quod in priore diximus libro, homo pro suae naturae modo sibi sit perfectionis ac foelicitatis auctor. Ordinum vero omnium supremus est sacerdotium, cui eucharistiae conficiendae potestas data est; insuper ligandi solvendique arbitrium. Episcopus vero tametsi non ipsius sacri ordinis causa, iurisdictione tamen est sacerdote superior. nam praeterquam quod potestatem [416] habet eucharistiae conficiendae, in qua verum Christi corpus continetur, in mysticum etiam corpus, id est in Ecclesiam iurisdictio eius longe lateque patet. horum vero quidam tantum Episcopi sunt, qui uni dumtaxat praesunt civitati: quidam Archiepiscopi, qui regioni et urbi metropoli, quibus Episcopi parere in nonnullis debent. superiores adhuc Archiepiscopis sunt Patriarchae. Omnium vero supremus est summus Pontifex, qui vicem Christi in terris gerit, dictusque est Papa per excellentiam quandam vocabulo a veteribus tam Graecis quam Latinis usurpato, quasi pater patrum Episcoporum.

---

[18] This word is not found in V 28v or in O 18r.
[19] V 28v and O 18r have "Nisi eis" etc.

sisted by constant nourishment, so likewise the sacrament of the most holy eucharist was established as kindling for the divine fire. By it all the virtues are kept warm and nourished by the life-giving flesh of Christ, and they always urge man on to higher and better things. Very often burdensome sicknesses that harm the body come about. There is need for the constant help of a medicine for them. Thus it frequently happens in the Christian life that practically all divine grace is utterly destroyed by the stain of sins. The sacrament of penance was instituted as a ready medicine against this deadly disease. The same pattern that doctors employ in purging out the leftovers of sickness by some gentle medicine is imitated by the Christian religion in man's spiritual life so that he may make use of a last anointing in leaving his mortal life, just as at the end of those sicknesses which keep on harassing and afflicting us as long as we go on living.

But since all followers of Christ, from whom the mystical Body of the Church (whose head is Christ) is made up as from [different] members, do not exist simultaneously, but some take over from others in life, it was necessary that the sacrament of matrimony and of the conjugal bed be established, which looks to the holy propagation of children. The sacrament of ecclesiastical orders is added to all of these as the last; [orders] were divinely established for providing spiritual birth, life and strength and also those medicines which we recounted above. As we said in the previous book, man in the measure of his own nature is the author of his own perfection and happiness. The priesthood is the highest of all the orders, for to it the power of consecrating the eucharist was given, in addition to the decision to bind and loose. The bishop is indeed still higher than the priest in his jurisdiction, even though not by reason of his sacred order itself. For besides his having the power of consecrating the eucharist, in which the true body of Christ is contained, his jurisdiction stretches far and wide also in the mystical body, that is, in the Church. Among them some are only bishops, who are in charge of only one city, some are archbishops who [are in charge] of a region and a metropolitan city; bishops should obey them in some things. Still higher than the archbishops are the patriarchs. Above all of them is the supreme pontiff, who takes the place of Christ on earth, and through a certain excellence he is called Pope, a term employed by both the Greeks and Latins of old, as though he were the father of the bishops, who are

Nam si quilibet princeps recte imperans paternam nuncupationem meretur; quanto magis Episcopo urbem christiana pietate moderanti nomen convenit patris?

Nos autem in priore libro Episcopum cum humanis tum divinis virtutibus instituimus. Nunc vero qua ratione sic institutus Episcopus, hisceque virtutibus ornatus exercere se in quibusve officiis versari debeat; pro virili persequemur. sed quoniam actiones circa singula quaedam sunt; praecepta quoque tradentur a nobis particularia magis quam in superiori libro fecimus. qua in re imitati pictorum solertiam videbimur, qui prius lineis quibusdam totam figuram informant ac comprehendunt; postmodum vero singulas partes effingunt lineamentis, coloribusque aptis ac propriis. eadem ratione nos quoque cum Episcopum virtutibus omnibus veluti primis lineis adumbraverimus; nunc explicandum ducimus, quo nam pacto in cuiuscunque virtutis munere, quod ad Episcopum pertineat, recte versari queat. principio quia charitas, veluti princeps virtutum omnium existit, si per singula charitatis officia discurremus, nihil utique a nobis omissum, quod ad hoc negotium spectet, iure videbitur. primum ergo, ne a recto ordine veluti de via deflectat oratio, persequenda sunt a nobis officia, quae pertinent ad divinum cultum. proxima his erunt illa, quae impendi debent in gubernatione ac curatione christiani gregis, iuxta Christi vitam ac mores. haec sequentur beneficentiae officia, et liberalitates, quibus uti Episcopum decet in levanda ac fovenda inopum hominum egestate. postremo qua ratione et exigi et impendi debeant redditus Episcopatus. his explicatis (ut reor) satis commode ac diligentur tractatum erit de omnibus Episcopi officiis.

Divinus cultus praeter interiorem animi habitum, de quo plura superius a nobis sunt dicta, primum requirit ab Episcopo, sicut a quovis sacerdote, ut quotidie divinas laudes, ac preces, quae in Ecclesiastico officio continentur, dicat magna in Deum animi intentione (utor autem usitata officii appellatione, quae quidem ab ea re deducta est, quod praecipuum sacerdotis officium sit, quotidie divinas eas laudes narrare) neque aliena animo verset, cum divinas laudes canit. verum omni conatu nitatur, ut ea, quae verbis promit, et intelligat, et quodam veluti animi gustu, si fieri possit, attingat.

themselves fathers. For if any prince who rules rightly merits a paternal title, how much more does the name of father befit a bishop who guides a city by his Christian piety?

In the previous book we taught the bishop both human and divine virtues. Now we will try as best we can to show how the bishop so trained and endowed with these virtues ought to conduct himself and in which duties he should be occupied. But because actions deal with individual cases, we shall lay down more specific precepts than we did in the previous book. On this matter we will be seen as having imitated the practice of painters, who first sketch and lay out the whole figure with some lines, and afterwards model the individual parts by fitting and proper lines and colors. In the same way, when we shall have sketched the bishop with all the virtues, as if with first strokes, we also think we now have to explain how he can rightly practice all the various virtues in the office which pertains to a bishop. It will seem right if at the outset we discourse about the individual duties of charity because charity stands out like the chief of all the virtues; thus we will rightly be esteemed as omitting nothing pertinent to this business. First, then, lest our discourse seem to diverge from the right order, as if from a path, we should examine the duties which pertain to divine worship. Next to these will be those duties which should be employed in governing and caring for the Christian flock, in accord with Christ's life and practice. These are followed by the duties of kindness and generosity which befit a bishop to use in relieving and helping the need of poor people. Lastly [comes] the rationale by which the income of the bishopric ought to be raised and expended. In my opinion, after these have been explained, all the duties of a bishop will have been covered with sufficient detail and care.

Aside from the interior disposition of the soul, about which we had much to say above, divine worship demands first of the bishop, as of any priest, that he daily say the divine praises and prayers, which are contained in the church office, with a soul very intent on God (I am using the usual terminology for his office, which derives from the fact that the main duty of a priest is to recite daily those divine praises); nor should he turn over in his mind unrelated subjects when he sings the divine praises. Indeed, he should bend every effort so that he both understands and as far as possible attends with a certain relish of soul to the things his words

mira certe huiusce intentionis vis est, si probis ac piis viris credimus, et ea, quam nullus, nisi experiatur, crediderit. commodius vero hoc assequetur, si non continenter totum divinum officium dixerit, sed per partes, aptis, convenientibusque diei horis, adeo ut diei partibus singulis reddantur officii portiones eae, quae sancto[20] quodam instituto illis accommodatae fuere. Nam [417] diuturnae lectionis taedio mens affecta, plerumque potius fastidio gravatur ac deprimitur, quam ad sublimiora attollatur; praeterquam quod sic per partes divinas laudes dici debere, et Propheta ipse in psalmo innuit. septies namque in die, inquit, laudem dixi tibi, et preces atque hymni singulis portionibus accommodati palam explicant.

quamobrem vellem ego (ut ab initio tandem ordiar diei ad exitum usque Episcopum perducturus) ut Episcopus in civitate fidei suae commissa residens (hoc namque eum praestare oportere supra diximus) antelucanis horis e cubili surgeret, matutinique laudes caneret, ei namque diei horae hymni ac preces matutini fuere accommodatae: propheta quoque dicit, media nocte surgebam ad confitendum tibi. his accedit peropportunum esse id tempus, idque silentium divinorum contemplationi; nec non etiam matutinam eam vigiliam mirifice prodesse bonae corporis valetudini, si Aristoteli credimus in oeconomicis id dicenti: post matutini laudes cum aurora instat, ambiguaque inter diem ac noctem est hora, quam maxime optarem, quando tunc et corpus somno penitus solutum est, et mens divinarum laudum narratione erecta, ut id temporis impenderetur orationi, quae sine vocis ullius strepitu sola mentis erectione meditationeque in Deum fieri solet.

---

[20] This word is missing in V 31v and O 19r.

express. There is certainly a marvelous power in this kind of attention, if we believe upright and devout men, and nobody would believe such things unless he had experienced them. This will be better achieved if he shall not have recited the whole divine office at a stretch, but by its parts at the right and fitting hours of the day, so that in the specific parts of the day those parts of the office are performed which were fitted to them by a certain sacred arrangement. For a mind influenced by boredom over the prolonged reading is generally weighed down and depressed by distaste rather than lifted up to more lofty things. Besides that, this is the way that the divine praises should be said in sections, as the Prophet himself suggests in the Psalm. For he says, "Seven times a day I praise thee" [Ps 119:164], and the prayers and hymns, which are adapted to the individual parts [of the day], clearly make explicit.[35]

Hence I would prefer (so that I may begin by leading the bishop from the beginning of the day all the way till its conclusion) that the bishop reside in the city entrusted to his charge (for we said above that he should do this) and should rise from his bed in the predawn hours and chant the morning praises, for the morning hymns and prayers were designed for that hour of the day: the Prophet also says, "At midnight I rise to praise thee" [Ps 119:62]. Added to these [considerations] is the fact that that time and that silence are very suited to the contemplation of things divine. And also that early morning vigil helps marvelously toward the good health of the body, if we believe Aristotle who says this in his *Economics*.[36] After morning praises, when dawn is about to break, there is an hour halfway between day and night. I would very much like it if, at the time when the body is then completely free from sleep and the mind has been aroused by the recounting of the divine praises, that time be devoted to the sort of prayer which is usually made without the clamor of any voice but only with the attention and meditation of the mind toward

---

[35] The Divine Office, which monks and friars were required to sing and priests and bishops to recite each day, consisted of seven hours or periods of prayer: matins, lauds, prime, terce, sext, none, and vespers. To these were added a night prayer, compline. Most of the Office was drawn from the Psalms.

[36] "Getting up before dawn is conducive to good health, prosperity, and wisdom": Aristotle, *Oeconomica*, I, 6 (1345a). Ben Franklin's version is more catchy: "Early to bed, early to rise makes a man healthy, wealthy and wise."

Nulla ratione fax maior menti adhiberi potest, quam hac animi excitatione. ex qua perhibent viri sanctitate ac religione insignes interdum cordi influere tam magnam divinorum, ac claram adeo intelligentiam, ut non amplius intelligendi modo consueto, sed aliena quadam ab homine ratione Deus menti adesse sentiatur; tantumque excitari in animo divini amoris ardorem, ut nihil aliud quam Deum mens sic affecta cogitare queat, neque se ipsam, nedum alia sentire, cum Deum sentiat. satis explicari oratione ulla non posset quantum intellectui luminis, quantumque virium ac roboris menti accedet ex hac divini radii illustratione. Nil vel abstrusissimum non intelligere, nulli quamvis arduae provinciae non satis esse potest mens tali fulgore perstricta. Hoc vero in munere humilem submissumque animum servet, neque mente assequi speret divinum illud arcanum ab omni eo remotissimum, quod mens hominum capere possit. Nam, ut in sacris literis traditur, qui perscrutator est maiestatis opprimetur a gloria. neque ad satietatem morari in huiuscemodi contemplatione eum velim, ex qua plerunque fastidium ac torpor animi solet oriri. quamobrem si se quandoque senserit ingenio ad eam orationem inepto esse, nolim ut quicquam moliatur invita (ut aiunt) Minerva, id est, repugnante natura: sed ea temporis hora se ad studia conferat, quae vel sint sacrarum literarum vel cuiuspiam alterius, quod ad sacras literas attineat. Nam impudica quaedam studia, nonnullasque superstitiosas disciplinas, ut magiam divinandique peritiam sive ex astris sive ex huiusmodi quopiam, non solum aliena putet, atque adversantia Episcopi studiis et offico: verum etiam pro virili nitatur ut penitus expellantur e civitate ea, cui praeest, cum vero iam dies illuxerit, solisque radiis fuerint reserata tenebrarum involucra, tunc primae diei horae laudes Deo concinat, quibus si volverit tertiae

God.[37] There is no way that a greater torch can be set to the mind than by this arousal of the soul. From this experience men outstanding for their holiness and devotion sometimes maintained that so great and clear an understanding of divine things sometimes floods into their heart that God is felt to be present to their mind no longer by the usual manner of understanding but by a certain way of thinking foreign to man. Such a great flame of divine love is stirred up in the soul that the mind so touched can think about nothing except God; it is unaware of itself, much less of anything else, while it is aware of God. No speech can fully explain how much light for the intellect and how much strength and power for the mind comes from this illumination of the divine ray. The mind gripped by such a flash cannot fail to understand anything, no matter how abstruse, nor is it unequal to any task, however difficult. In this task let him preserve a humble and submissive soul; let him not hope to attain by his mind that divine secret which is utterly removed from all that the human mind can grasp. For as is handed down in the sacred scriptures, the person who is a searcher of majesty is overwhelmed by glory.[38] I would not want him to tarry in this sort of contemplation unto satiety, for this usually gives rise to distaste and sluggishness of soul. Therefore should he at times feel that he is of scant talent for that prayer, I would not want him laboring at anything "against the will of Minerva" (as they say), that is, when nature is rebellious. Rather for that hour of time he should devote himself to studies, whether they be about the sacred scriptures or something else which relates to the sacred scriptures. May he regard, not only as foreign to but as opposed to a bishop's endeavors and duty, certain shameful studies and some superstitious disciplines such as magic and skill at divination, whether from the stars or from anything of that sort. Rather he should also strive with all his strength to drive them completely out of the city over which he presides. When the day has already shone forth and the curtains of darkness have been drawn back by the rays of the sun, then may he sing to God the praises of first hour of the day. If he should

---

[37] Morning meditation was encouraged by the *devotio moderna* before Contarini; during the Counter Reformation it took on great importance among pious Catholics. Rules and directions for systematic meditation were provided by writers such as St. Ignatius of Loyola and St. Francis de Sales. Several meditation manuals ran through hundreds of editions.

[38] Prov 25:27 in the Vulgate.

quoque laudes continenter annectere, nil puto fecerit reprehensione dignum.

ab his statim eucharistae sacra vel [418] ipse celebret, vel saltem singulis quibusque diebus illis intersit alio ea celebrante sacerdote. Non tamen committendum reor, quin frequenter, si minus quotidie, celebret sacra missarum, sanctissimumque eucharistiae Sacramentum, et conficiat et sumat. Nam cum hoc cuilibet sacerdoti faciendum incumbat; ne sit Deo parum gratus pro sacerdotii dignitate, neve intermissione tantae oblationis vivorum mortuorumque animas levare cesset, aut parum lubenti animo dominicae mortis memoriam colat; tum maxime ad Episcopum videtur hoc pertinere, qui cum sacerdos sit, purgatissimo etiam animo esse debet, et divinae illustrationi undique pervio.[21] quod maxime assequetur frequenti illius Sacramenti oblatione atque usu. quo fit ut improbandam quorundam Episcoporum consuetudinem rear, qui raro admodum ad participationem mensae coelestis accedunt. Vidi ego Petrum Barocium Episcopum Patavinum, virum, qui nunquam satis pro meritis laudari queat, quotidie, cum primum dies illuxerat, in privato quodam sacello missarum solemnia celebrantem eximia sanctitate animique intentione in Deum. idem quoque factitasse plerosque probos Episcopos memoriae proditum est, qui ex frequenti huius Sacramenti usu assequebantur, ut aptissimo perspicacique admodum ingenio essent ad abstrusissima quaeque scripturarum loca intelligenda, efficacique ac vivida oratione facillime christianam quemque ad suscipiendam vitam et mores christianos impellerent.[22] Nam, ut inquit Propheta in psalmo, memoriam suavitatis tuae eructabunt.

his peractis, quae tum ad divinum cultum, tum etiam ad animi erectionem quandam faciunt; tertia iam diei hora instante, conferet se Episcopus noster ad eos excipiendos, atque audiendos, qui ipsum vel tanquam iudicem, vel tanquam consultorem, vel tanquam

---

[21] The Paris editor has considerably revised the last two sentences. In both V 33rv and O 20r they read as follows: "Non tamen omittendum reor, quin frequenter, si non quotidie sacra celebret missarum, eucharistiaeque Sacramentum, et conficiat et assumat. Nam quum cuilibet sacerdoti hoc faciendum incumbat; ne videatur Deo parum gratus pro sacerdotii dignitate, ne non parum lubenti animo appareat dominicae mortis memoriam colere, tum maxime episcopi hoc interesse videtur, qui praeterquam sacerdos sit, purgatissimo etiam animo esse debet, et indique divinae pervio illustrationi."

[22] In both V 34r and O 20v the end of this sentence reads: "... facillime cuique vitam et mores imitandos persuaderet."

desire to add on immediately the praises of terce, he will in my view do nothing worthy of criticism.

Right after these let him personally celebrate the sacred [rites] of the eucharist or at least every single day attend them with some other priest as celebrant. Still I don't think that this should be delegated; rather, frequently if not daily he should celebrate the sacred rites of the Mass and consecrate and consume the most holy sacrament of the eucharist. For since every priest has an obligation to perform this, lest he be insufficiently grateful to God for the dignity of the priesthood, or lest he cease to edify souls by discontinuing such a great oblation for the living and the dead, or lest he should honor the memory of the Lord's death with a heart too little enthusiastic, then [celebrating Mass] seems to pertain to a bishop above all, who since he is a priest should have a very clean heart and should be everywhere open to divine illumination. This is best achieved by frequently offering and using that sacrament. Thus it happens that I think that the practice of some bishops deserves criticism, who very rarely come forward to participate at the heavenly table. I myself saw Pietro Barozzi, the bishop of Padua, a man who can never be praised enough for his merits, celebrating daily the solemn rites of Mass in some private chapel at day's first light with great holiness, his soul intent on God.[39] The remembrance has been handed down of how very many upright bishops did the same thing; by the frequent use of this sacrament they attained this—that they possess a very precise and probing gift for understanding all the most hidden scripture passages and they urged everybody by effective and vivid preaching to undertake readily Christian living and behavior. For as the Prophet says in the Psalm [145:7], "They shall pour forth the fame of thy abundant goodness."

After having performed these acts which contribute both to divine worship and toward uplifting of the soul, as the third hour of the day comes on, let our bishop devote himself to receiving and listening to those who come to him either as a judge or as a counsel-

---

[39] Barozzi was bishop of Padua from 1487 to 1507 and was well known to Contarini and his friends Tommaso Giustiniani and Vincenzo Querini from their years as students at Padua. Gigliola Fragnito urges that Barozzi's example strongly influenced Contarini's thinking on the conduct of a model bishop: *Gasparo Contarini*, 137-140.

adiutorem adibunt; quibus se facilem, benignumque praebeat, ita tamen ne a gravitate recedat. Expediat statim quae potest, recte, iusteque iudicet, consulentibus fidum consilium det, opemque ferat quibus poterit; nec ab hoc munere cesset, quousque omnes audierit. hoc enim officium quibuscunque aliis praeferendum duco; dimittat vero, quantum fieri possit, omnes a se laetos, tristem nullum. quod si non poterit, conetur saltem humana, lenique oratione mitigare eorum tristitiam, animique turbationem. non tamen praeterea committendum puto; ut non interdum virorum improborum ac pervicacium, quos si lenius tractes magis exasperes, contumaciam retundat asperis gravibusque verbis; quibus profecto parentes in filios, quos maxime amant, uti quandoque solent. Haec vero omnia quam optime praestabit, si vera, non autem ficta charitate praeditus fuerit, suaeque fidei commissos amaverit tanquam filios. probe enim in omnibus hisce officiis ab ea erudietur virtute.

non me latet plerosque Episcopos haec munera vicario delegare: quod (ut reor) ex mollitie quadam animi faciunt: ne scilicet horum negotiorum impedimentis interpellantur, ne animo queant operam dare. Vacationem hanc, rerumque procurationem per Vicarium numquam ego laudaverim; nisi Episcopus vel incommoda corporis valetudine, aut cuiuspiam alterius officii occupatione, quod sine reprehensione omitti non [419] possit, impeditus, operam ipse suam praestare nequeat. non tamen alienum esse puto, ut Episcopus vicarium habeat virum aliquem doctum, ac probum, cuius opera utatur in plerisque. Nam si multitudine negotiorum oppressus ad omnia expedienda satis ipse non esset; vel si longinqua loca essent adeunda, ad quae satis commode nequiret ipse accedere; in hisce huiusmodique officiis vicarii opera uti, et decorum et necessarium

lor or as a helper. Let him make himself affable and kindly to them, but not so as to lessen his dignity. Let him handle immediately the things he can, judge rightly and fairly, give trustworthy advice to those seeking counsel, and give help to those he can. He should not break off this duty until he shall have heard everybody. I feel this duty should take priority over all others. As far as he can, let him send away from him everybody happy and nobody sad. But if this is impossible, at least he should try to ease their sadness and troubled heart with gentle speech. Still, I do not think it should be ruled out that he may sometimes blunt the obstinacy of wicked and stubborn men, whom you render more harsh the more gently you treat them, with the hard and severe words which parents, indeed, are sometimes wont to use with their children whom they love very much. He will do all these things the best possible way if he shall have been endowed with a true and unfeigned charity and shall have loved like sons those committed to his trust. That virtue will teach him rightly about all these duties.

The fact that most bishops delegate these tasks to a vicar is not hidden from me. In my opinion they do this out of a certain weakness—namely lest the difficulties from these engagements interrupt them so that they cannot give attention to their soul. I will never praise this evasion and the handling of business through a vicar except when the bishop, hindered and personally unable to carry on his work either because of bad physical health or by preoccupation with some other duty which he cannot omit without censure, is unable to perform his office personally.[40] Still, I do not think it inconsistent that the bishop have as vicar some learned and upright man whose labor he uses in many things. If he is weighed down by the number of his engagements and is not himself capable of handling everything, or if there is need to travel to many distant places which he cannot himself fairly easily reach, it is fitting and almost necessary to

---

[40] Absentee bishops were a major curse of the Pre-Tridentine church. The question of episcopal residence and whether it was of *ius divinum* was one of the most bitterly disputed points at the Council of Trent: Hubert Jedin, *A History of the Council of Trent*, (New York: Nelson, 1961) II, 317-69. Contarini himself never resided in his diocese of Belluno, not by choice, but because Paul III needed his presence in Rome to encourage reform, at Regensburg to negotiate with the Lutherans, and finally at Bologna as legate and chief administrator of the second city of the papal states.

prope est. Post peracta negotia iterum ad divinas laudes revertatur, sextamque ac nonam dicat. his nanque laudibus ea propemodum diei hora conveniet.

post id, si volet, se ad prandium conferat: in quo sordes non laudo, magnificum vero apparatum et vasorum et ciborum, ministrorumque copiam et nimiam lautitiam summopere vitupero. Nam per *Deos* {Deum} quid magis alienum a natura rerum conspici potest, quam pastorem christiani gregis, cui vita Christi tanquam exemplar proposita sit, epulis emancipatum videre, eaque ipsa facientem ac perpetrantem, quae in aliis vituperare ac corrigere in primis ille ipse debet?[23] praeterea quid magis indecens, quam reditus Episcopatus, quos probi viri olim legarunt ad divinum cultum augendum et ad levandam egentium inopiam, in magnis coenarum apparatibus atque gulae ingluvie profundi?[24] erit ergo Episcopi prandium non sordidum, parcum tamen, ut magis naturae necessitati quam gulae voluptati consultum videatur. sed ne illo etiam tempore cibi voluptate penitus capiantur, magnopere laudo quorundam consuetudinem, qui semper prandio coenaeve divinam aliquam adhibent lectionem: ex qua duplicem fructum meo iudicio reportant. Nam primum, ut dicebam, erigitur animus, ne voluptate cibi prematur, simulque cavetur, ne fiat lapsus in scurriles iocos, quod interdum inter coenandum accidere solet. quibus omnibus optime puto consultum iri, si divina lectio adhibeatur, si non toti praedio coenaeve, attamen maximae parti. post prandium iocari aliquantulum liceat cum familiaribus, qui aderunt, dummodo iocus neque in contumeliam alicuius, neque in obscoenitatem labatur. verum et scurrilitas summopere vitanda, et in lepore orationis quam maxime servanda est gravitas. Risus quoque immodicus cohibendus.

Neque reprehenderim aliquod musicae genus. liberalissimam nanque relaxationem censuerim ex musica animo adhiberi: sed cum valde afficiatur animus harmonia, multumque valeat et ad sedandas, et ad excitandas perturbationes, nec non ad mores animi componendos, diligentissime observandum duco, quod etiam inter

---

[23] In place of "eaque ... debet?" both V 35v and O 21r have "idque ipsum praestare quod in aliis vitupere ac corrigere maxime debeat?"

[24] Here both V 35v and O 21r have: "ad levandam egenorum inopiam Christianorum, in magnis coenarum apparatibus atque gulae ingluvie sumptitari?"

use the labor of a vicar in these sorts of duties. After completing these appointments, let him again turn back to the divine praises and say sext and none. For that hour of the day is just about right for these praises.

After this, if he wishes, let him betake himself to dinner, in which I do not praise parsimony but I strongly condemn a brilliant array of dishes and foods and a crowd of servants and excessive elegance. For by *the gods* {God} what can appear more contrary to the nature of things than to see a shepherd of the Christian flock, for whom the life of Christ serves as a model, given up to banqueting and doing and committing the very things that he himself should be the first to excoriate and correct in others? Moreover, what is more improper than lavishing the income of the bishopric, which upright men once bequeathed to enrich divine worship and relieve the poverty of the needy, on a great array of dinners and the gluttony of the palate. Therefore the bishop's dinner will be not niggardly but sparing, so that he may seem to have consulted the needs of nature more than the pleasure of the palate. But lest they seem to be completely engrossed in the pleasure of food even at that time, I greatly praise the practice of certain people who always make use of some divine reading for dinner and supper—in my judgement they gain a twofold profit from this. As I was saying, first the soul is uplifted lest it be oppressed by the pleasure of food, and at the same time precaution is taken against falling into scurrilous jokes, which sometimes is wont to happen during dining. I think all of them are best advised to make use of a sacred reading at least in the larger part if not in the whole of dinner or supper. After dinner it is all right to joke for a short time with the friends who are present provided that the joking descend neither into making fun of somebody nor into obscenity. But buffoonery is to be utterly avoided and during pleasant conversation gravity is to be preserved as much as possible. Likewise excessive laughter is to be restrained.

I would not object to some kind of music either. For I would judge that the soul gains its most liberating relaxation from music, but since the soul is deeply touched by harmony, and since it has great power to calm or arouse our emotions and likewise to soothe the soul's behavior, I think very carefully attention should be paid to

Ethnicos[25] Aristoteles philosophorum princeps monuit in politicis, et Plato in plerisque prodidit locis, ne Episcopi aures, ac per eas animus assuescat mollibus quibusdam cantus ac soni harmoniis, quibus vel robustissimi animi vigor molliri obtundive queat, et ad libidines excitari: neque rursus Phrygius ille harmoniae modus est admittendus, quo in furorem hominum mentes plerunque aguntur; quo in genere, nostris temporibus rarius peccatur, frequentissime vero in priori: sed solida quaedam constansque musica recipienda est: qua animum oblectare liberalis atque ingenui est viri, dummodo ne tota teratur dies in huiusmodi oblectatione.

Nam iocus atque animi relaxatio ad [420] negotia, actionesque serias referenda est, ut scilicet animus alacrior factus ex ioco in quavis functione melius versari queat. quo fit ut postquam id temporis iocis impensum fuerit, quod satis esse videbitur et ad animi relaxationem, et ad bonum valetudinm corporis, continuo ad seria redeundum sit, ac siqua negotia incumbent, danda opera est, ut conficiantur. si quid vero supererit temporis: vel consuetudinibus amicorum, vel literarum studiis est id omne impendendum, colloquia vero cum amicis a tenore vitae discrepari nequaquam debent. sint igitur de rebus christianis, aut de re aliqua, quae ad bonos mores, vel ad studia literarum pertineat. Hoc etenim cum eruditis ac probis viris consuetudinis genus magni studii interdum vicem gerit ac praestat.[26] multa namque plerunque ab amicis, veluti ex vivis libris, decerpimus. quae magis inhaerere animo quandoque solent, quam ea, quae ex librorum discimus lectione. Nollem tamen propterea quempiam suspicari, laudare nos morosum quoddam ac grave consuetudinis genus: immo quam maxime fieri possit affabilitatem ac facilitatem adhibendam esse censemus.

<hr />

[25] V 36r and O 21v lack "inter Ethnicos."
[26] V 37r and O 22r have "supplet" for "gerit ac praestat."

what, even among the pagans, Aristotle (the prince of philosophers) warned about in his *Politics*[41] and what Plato suggested in several places,[42] lest the bishop's ears and through them his soul should become accustomed by certain gentle harmonies of song and sound which could soften or blunt the vigor of the even the stoutest soul and stir up its passions. Again, that Phrygian mode of harmony ought not to be allowed, which drives the minds of most men to fury. This kind of sin happens rather rarely in our times, but earlier it was very common. We should welcome a solid and steady sort of music, which gives enjoyment to the soul of a noble and honorable man, provided only that the whole day is not squandered in this sort of enjoyment.[43]

Jesting and mental relaxation should be related to business and serious activity, that is, so that the soul, made more keen from jesting, can engage in any task more effectively. Thus it happens that, after spending in jesting what will seem sufficient time for relaxing the soul and for the good health of the body, one should immediately return to serious tasks, and if there is some pressing business, care should be taken so that it be accomplished. If some time shall be left over, all of it should be spent in companionship with friends or in literary pursuits; conversations with friends surely should never be split off from one's pattern of life. Let them then deal with Christian concerns or with something else which is related to good behavior or literary pursuits. This sort of companionship with learned and upright men sometimes takes the place of and is better than hard study. For oftentimes we acquire much from our friends, as if from living books. These things are sometimes wont to stick in our mind more than those things that we learn by reading books. Still I would not want anybody thereby to suspect that we praise some morose or solemn sort of conversations; indeed, we think that affability and friendliness should be used as far as possible.

---

[41] Aristotle deals with the role of music in education in his *Politics*, VIII, 5 (1339-1342). He discusses the Phrygian mode in 1342b.

[42] Plato, *Republic*, III, 398E-402; see also 410-411. In contrast to Contarini, Plato retains only the Dorian and Phrygian modes, which for him represented courage and sobriety. Contarini's opposition to the Phrygian mode should not be taken in a technical sense; what he really opposes is music that will stir rather than soothe the emotions.

[43] Contarini's correspondence notes the pleasure he took from music and the company of friends: Gleason, 23. His *De magistratibus et republica Venetorum*, first published at Paris in 1543 but started about 1523, uses musical harmony as a metaphor for a well-ordered civil government: Gleason, 117.

At cum in occasum inclinat dies ad divinas laudes revertendum est: ne in postrema diei hora tanquam abortum fecisse videamur. dicendae ergo sunt vespertinae laudes, dirigendaque mens in Deum, quibus si completorium, hoc est ultimam officii portionem coniunxerit; non ab re facturum puto. quod si postremam hanc partem post coenam, cum cubile petiturus est, dixerit: satis arbitror tempestive id faciet. Reliquum vero temporis, quod a vesperis ad coenam usque pertinet; vellem, ni aliud obstiterit, lectioni ac studiis impendi, quae cuiusmodi futura sint, satis supra a nobis est dictum. in coena eundem morem servet, quem in prandio servavit, ut et parca sit coena, et divina lectio adhibeatur, et urbanitate concludatur, ac musica, si lubebit. valde tamen proderit, si maiori utatur in coena, quam in prandio, abstinentia cibi. Nam et leniorem somnum ducet, et alacrior erit ad matutinam vigiliam. quorum utrunque impedit stomachus nimio cibo gravatus. Hanc fere vitae seriem Episcopo servandam esse arbitramur, nullum tamen propterea opinari vellem ita hunc ordinem vivendi a nobis institui, ut et omnibus et semper servandum esse ducamus. quin potius censemus fieri non posse, ut humanae actiones in re quapiam certa quadam regula concludantur. sed utendum esse remur in humanis actionibus regula Lesbia, id est, plumbea, flexili inquam, non rigida, ut scilicet pro conditione temporum ac personarum flecti, deduci, ac reduci queat. sic igitur in hoc quoque negotio pro temporum occasione ac rerum, pro personarum ingenio, et flecti et reduci regula haec poterit a nobis praescripta.

Nihil enim prohibet, si quando rus ex urbe secesserit, ut nonnullis honestissimis exercitationibus[27] per aliquot dies operam det, recreandi animi causa, alium vitae morem servare. siqua etiam vel negotii conficiendi occasio, vel amici adventus intervenerit, deesse utique officio non debet, nec praescriptam vivendi normam deserere. difficile vero

---

[27] V 38r and O 22v have "aucupiis venationibusque" for "nonnullis honestissimis exercitationibus."

But when the day inclines toward sunset, we should return to praising God lest we might be seen as if aborting the last hour of the day. Therefore the praises at vespers should be said and our mind directed toward God; I think it would not be inappropriate if compline, that is, the last part of the office, were joined to these [prayers]. But if he were to say this last part after supper, when he was preparing for bed, I regard him as doing it at an appropriate enough hour. The remaining time, which falls between vespers and supper, I would like to have spent, if something does not prevent it, in reading and study—we have said enough above about the sort of things they will be. At supper let him keep up the same practice as he followed at dinner, so that the supper be sparing and a sacred reading be employed, and let it close with a friendly exchange or with music, if that pleases. Still it will be very profitable if greater restraint in eating is employed at supper than at dinner. For he will sleep more peacefully, and he will more prompt at the morning vigil. A stomach weighted down with too much food presents a problem in both cases. We think that the bishop should keep up roughly this pattern of life, but I would not want anybody to conclude from this that this order of living was set up by us as something we think everybody ought always to observe. On the contrary, we feel that it is impossible that human actions be restricted on any point by some fixed rule. But we think that in human actions we should use the Lesbian rule,[44] that is, a leaden rule, flexible and not rigid, I say, one such that it can be bent and adapted and readapted to the condition of the times and persons. Thus in this business too this rule which we have prescribed will be susceptible to bending and readapting depending on the times, circumstances and the make-up of the persons.

There is nothing to prevent him keeping up a different pattern of life if sometimes he leaves the city for a retreat in the countryside, so that for some days he may devote himself to some respectable exercises to refresh his soul.[45] Should an opportunity for completing business or a visit by a friend intervene, he should not neglect his duty nor desert his prescribed manner of living. The bishop will find

---

[44] The Lesbian rule was a mason's rule made of lead so that it could be bent to fit and measure curved surfaces: see Aristotle, *Nicomachean Ethics*, V. 10. (1137b 30).

[45] Contarini himself delighted in vacations at his country villa, Gleason, 25.

in huiusmodi officiis sese continere Episcopus poterit; nisi eam sibi familiam paret, quae et vitae probitate sit insignis, nec bonas artes aspernetur, quod ipsum etiam maxime spectare [421] puto ad decorem Episcopi. Nam familiaris, qui pravis sit moribus, et universam familiam domi perturbat, et foris maximo plerunque dedecore afficit. quare magna illi adhibenda est diligentia, ne quaepiam in familiam admittat, qui probitate conspicuus non sit. Hac enim ratione tum quietam domi vitam aget, tum etiam male foris non audiet; quod maxime Episcopo cavendum est, non tantum sui commodi gratia, quantum ne civibus suis noceat malo exemplo.

Natura enim comparatum est; ut imitatione praesulum quodcunque sibi licere caeteri homines putent, ac illud quoque non est negligendum, ne aliquam familiam sibi adsciscat, quae malis quidem moribus non sit; sed tamen suspicionem iure afferre possit malae cuiuspiam artis, vel de se vel de domino, vel de quopiam alio famliari. qua in re perpulchram mehercle sententiam plane Caesare dignam sequetur, qui cum uxorem dimisisset ex suspicione tantum stupri cum Clodio, coniugem, inquit Caesaris non solum culpa, sed etiam suspicione culpae, vacare oportet. Sic Episcopus ac multo magis, cum eius vita velut exemplar aliis proposita sit, non tantum macula, verum etiam omni vel levissima suspicione maculae carere debet. Danda ipsi etiam opera erit, ut familiam quam probam elegerit, in officio contineat, atque unumquenque familiarium pro meritorum, ac virtutum magnitudine ad maiorem promoveat dignitatis gradum. ea vero ratione et victui et vestitui consulet domesticorum, ut nec dignitas Episcopatus neglecta, nec luxuria aut pompa ulla adhibita esse videatur.

familiarium vero, cum aegrotant, magnam habeat curam, provideatque eo pacto illorum incolumitati, ut neque impensae, nec cuiuspiam incommodi ratio habita fuisse videatur. memini ego, dum Patavii agerem, Petrum Barocium, de quo supra dixi,[28] insignem Episcopum, constantissime hoc servasse, praeterquam quod aegrotis familiaribus omnia suppeditarentur, quibus erat

---

[28] V 39v and O 23r do not have "de quo supra dixi."

it difficult to confine himself to duties of this sort unless he builds himself a household [of subordinates] who are outstanding for upright life and do not spurn the belle arts. This is also something which in my view contributes much to the bishop's reputation. For a servant who has wicked habits disturbs the whole household at home and most often brings great disgrace on it aboard. Therefore he must employ great care lest he admit into his household anybody who is not conspicuous for his probity. On this basis he will have a quiet life at home and also will not be denigrated abroad. This above all the bishop must guard against, not so much for his own sake, as to avoid harming his fellow citizens by bad example.

Nature has ordained that the rest of men think that anything at all is permissible to them in imitation of superiors; this point must not be overlooked lest he admit into his household any persons who, although not having bad morals, might rightly arouse suspicion of any evil practice either regarding themselves, or their master, or any other subordinate. On this point, by Hercules, he will follow the very apt statement which was indeed worthy of Caesar, who divorced his wife on the mere suspicion of defilement by Clodius. "The wife of Caesar," he said, "should be free of not only fault but even the suspicion of fault."[46] The same applies even more to a bishop since his life is held up as an example to others; he ought to be free not only from stain but also every suspicion, even the slightest, of stain. He will have to try hard to select an upright household [of subordinates], to retain them in their positions, and promote individuals from his household according to the greatness of their merits and virtues to positions of greater dignity. For this reason he will take heed of the food and clothing of his servants so that it may be evident that neither the dignity of episcopal rank has been slighted nor any luxury and display have been employed.

Let him devote great care to his subordinates when they fall sick and on that score let him look after their welfare in a way that does not seem to take account of expenses or any inconvenience. I recall that when I was living at Padua Pietro Barozzi, the outstanding bishop about whom I spoke above, kept unwaveringly to this point: that aside from providing his sick subordinates with everything they

---

[46] Plutarch, *Vita Caesaris* [12]; *The Fall of the Roman Republic: Six Lives*, translated by Rex Warner (New York: Penguin, 1972) 254.

opus, ne unquam Medicus sine ipso aegrotum inviseret. aderat ipse et consultationibus Medicorum et prognosticis. Hoc vero praestabat in singulos, ut ne postremos aut infimos neglexisse videretur. laudanda sane charitas, vereque Episcopo dignum officium. Consuetudo autem cum familiaribus tum gravitate, tum facilitate condita sit, ne scilicet vel despectui vel odio habeatur: sed ea utatur dexteritate, ut et verendum et charum sese familiaribus praebeat. satis dictum puto pro opusculi nostri brevitate de officiis Episcopi, quibus et divinum cultum servare, et se ac familiam in muneribus virtutum continere debeat.

Nunc quod secundo loco propositum erat; ea nobis officia exponenda sunt quae praestare Episcopum oportet in gubernatione gregis fidei suae commissi, quantum ad virtutes, ac vitam Christianam pertinet. Omnis civitatis multitudo in mares ac foeminas primo divisa est. marium porro quidam sacerdotes sunt, vel sacris initiati, alii prophani; mulieres item, quaedam Christo virginitatem voverunt, ac in coenobiis vivunt. reliquae aliud vitae genus elegerunt.[29] *prior* {potior} cura Episcopo de maribus esse debet, quam de foeminis, tum quia mares natura foeminis praestant, tum etiam, quoniam cum ordine quodam gubernatio procedat civitatis. foeminae natura sunt viris subiectae eorumque imperio praesto [422] esse debent. quare Episcopi regimen mediis viris veluti instrumentis quibusdam ad foeminas usque pertendi videtur. ac virorum quoniam quidam communi vitae Christianae ratione funguntur,[30] quidam vero sacris initiati sunt, eadem ratione clerici primum spectant ad curam Episcopi. Nam eis veluti ministris utatur oportet ad gregis reliqui moderationem.

In clericis vero hi, qui seculares laicive dicuntur, praeferendi itidem sunt iis, qui vulgo religiosi vocantur, qui propris quibusdam ducibus parent, et a civitatis grege seclusi esse videntur; clerici ergo ii adsciscuntur[31] ad Ecclesiasticos ordines ab Episcopo, et ab eo in officio contineri debent. principio igitur magna disquisitione; nec mediocri iudicio utatur opus est in promotione clericorum ad ordines

---

[29] V 40r and O 23v have "… vivunt, reliquae prophanae."

[30] In V 40v and O 23v this sentence reads, "ac virorum cum quidem prophani sunt, quidam …."

[31] In V 40v and O 23v this sentence reads, "In clericis vero hi, qui nulla religione obstricti sunt, adhuc praeferendi sunt religiosis, qui propris quibusdam ducibus parent, et a civitatis grege sequestrati esse videntur; clerici vero religione soliti et adsciscuntur" etc.

needed, the doctor never visited the sick person without him. He himself was present for all the consultations and diagnoses of the doctors. He did this for each and all, lest he seem to have been negligent about the last and most lowly.[47] His charity indeed deserves praise, as truly does his worthy performance as a bishop. Personal relationships with subordinates is founded on both gravity and friendliness, lest he be regarded with either contempt or hatred, but he should employ such skill that he shows himself to his subordinates as both to be feared and to be loved. I think I have said enough, given the brevity of this little book of ours, about a bishop's duties in which he should maintain divine worship and conduct himself and his household in the exercise of the virtues.

Now to the second subject that was proposed: we should explain those duties which a bishop ought to perform in governing the flock entrusted to his care insofar as it relates to the virtues and Christian living. First, the population of every city is divided into men and women. Of the men some are priests or have entered sacred orders, others are laymen; likewise some women have vowed virginity to Christ and live in convents. The rest have chosen a different manner of life. The bishop's *first* {greater} concern should be the men rather than the women, both because men by nature come before women and also because the government of the city proceeds in a certain order. By nature women should be subject to men and ready [to obey] their command. Hence the bishop's rule seems to reach out to women through men as intermediaries like certain instruments. Among the men, because some observe the Christian life by living in community and some have entered sacred orders, for that very reason the clergy have first call on the bishop's care. He should then make use of them as helpers in directing the rest of his flock.

Among the clergy those who are termed secular or lay are likewise to be put ahead of those who are commonly called religious, obey their own superiors, and seem separate from the city's flock. The clergy are approved for ecclesiastical orders by the bishop and ought to be maintained in office by him. There is then need for careful enquiry at the beginning, and need that he use extraordinary discretion in pro-

---

[47] Fragnito, *Gasparo Contarini*, 178n, suggests that Barozzi's concern about sick members of his household may also have been strongly motivated by his personal interest in medicine.

Ecclesiasticos. qua in re hac tempestate, meo quidem iudicio, gravissime fere omnes peccant, nullo enim discrimine habito et scelestissimi et maxime ignari omnium bonarum artium homines ad participationem divinae potestatis, quae est in sacerdotibus admittuntur. qui postmodum pollutis manibus, inquinatissimaque mente tractant quotidie ineffabile, ac omni veneratione dignissimum corporis Christi Sacramentum. in magnis autem sceleribus deprehensi Christianae rei maximum afferunt detrimentum. quibus tandem auctoribus praestitam sibi quoque eorum imitatione plebs licentiam putat[32] quodvis facinus perpetrandi. quo fit ut existimem magnam adhiberi diligentiam oportere, ne huiusmodi aliquod monstrum Episcopo, quem instituimus, auctore ad ordines Ecclesiasticos admittatur; quin potius eligantur viri et probis moribus ornati, et doctrina conspicui, ut idonei ministri Episcopo adesse queant in erudienda civitate Christiana religione, et bonis moribus excolenda.

Hoc in loco illud quoque obiter admonere in mentem venit, ne eos ullo pacto admittat ad ordinem Ecclesiasticum, qui potius ut impunitatem *peccandi* {peccati} habeant sacris initiandos se procurant, quam quod clerici esse velint. sunt inter hos plerunque viri genere nobiles, servili tamen ingenio: qui tanquam ad arcem scelerum, quae animo conceperunt, ad sacra ordinesque confugiunt. Hi penitus relegandi sunt a Sacramenti huius participatione. quod si quando accidat, ut horum aliquis in scelere deprehensus sese tutari velit, ne debitas poenas luat, sacri ordinis causa ope ab Episcopo implorata, nequaquam committat, me auctore, Episcopus, ut scelerum patrocinium ac iustitiae impedimentum sacra ordinesque esse velit. verum nisi omnia servaverit, quae is, qui sacris initiatus est, servare debet, tum vita, tum cultu, tum etiam toto habitu corporis, illum prophano praesidi puniendum tradat. Si vero obsisteret aliqua causa, propter quam tradendus non videretur iudici, legibusque civilibus: tunc iudex ipse severissimo utatur iudicio, ne Ecclesiam Christi Asylum facere videatur.

Sed redeat unde deflexit oratio. Parum quidem laboris reliquum erit Episcopo in cleri moderatione, si in electione clericorum non peccaverit. Nam facile in officio continebit eos qui statim ab ineunte

---

[32] V 40v and O 24r have "profani licentiam putant."

moting clerics to ecclesiastical orders. At this time, in my judgment, almost everybody sins seriously in this matter; without there being any discernment men who are infamous and utterly ignorant of all culture are admitted to partake in the divine power which belongs to priests. Soon they are daily handling with their soiled hands and filthy mind the ineffable sacrament of Christ's body, which is most worthy of all veneration. After they are caught in serious crimes they inflict enormous harm on the Christian cause. Finally, presented with such models, the common folk think that they too have been given license to imitate them in perpetrating any villainy. This is why I consider that the greatest diligence should be used to keep this sort of monster from being admitted to ecclesiastical orders by the bishop whom we have been instructing. Rather let men endowed with upright behavior and outstanding in learning be chosen so that they can assist the bishop as suitable ministers in educating the city in the Christian religion and cultivating good morals.

At this point this comes to mind in passing: let him under no conditions admit to ecclesiastical orders those who secure their admission to sacred orders so that they may have impunity *to sin* {for sin} rather than because they want to be clergy. There are many among them, noble by birth but having a slave disposition, who take refuge in their sacred roles and orders as a sort of citadel for the crimes they nurture in their heart. These men are to be completely kept away from participating in this sacrament. But if it should sometime happen that one of them is caught in a crime and wants to be protected lest he suffer well deserved punishments by begging for help from the bishop because of his sacred order, then the bishop in my view should not in the least allow himself to desire that sacred things and orders should serve as a shield for crimes and an impediment to justice. He should hand a person over to the secular official for punishment unless he shall have observed all that one initiated into sacred orders should observe, whether as regards his life or his worship, or even his whole physical comportment. If there is some ground which suggests that he should not be handed over to a judge and civil laws, then [the bishop] himself as judge should pass a very harsh sentence lest he seem to be making the Church of Christ into a place of refuge.

But let our discussion go back to where it digressed. If he has not sinned in choosing clergymen, there will be little work left the bishop in directing the clergy. For he will easily keep to their duty those who

aetate bonis artibus, probisque moribus fuerint instituti. iuniores ergo erudiendos curabit, non humanitatis, aut huiusmodi quibusdam studiis, nisi quantum sit satis; sed Christiana disciplina, [423] Theologia inquam, *non ea contentiosa ac pervicaci, ut ita dixerim, quae animum tumore quodam inflat, magnisque obest quam prosit; sed veterum theologorum disciplinis,* nec non etiam iure pontificio quod theologiae illi conveniat. *Nam contentiosum hoc ius quod circa sacerdotium iura litesque versatur, et ingeniose adinventum est ab adulatoribus plaerisque*[33] *clericorum (libere agam, ut res postulat) quoque permittitur, ut quidvis recte fieri posse videatur, non dicam amplius, non magni faciendum sane reor, in his vero locis penitus aspernandum, in quibus discrepant iurisconsulti nostrae tempestatis a priscis Theologis.* praeferenda tamen omnibus sunt studia sacrae scripturae, quae absolutionem tandem imponant quibuslibet clericorum studiis. Haec volumina semper in manibus esse debent, ut quod Flaccus dicit de auctoribus Graecis, dicamus nos de sacris,

> vos o sacerdotes volumina sacra nocturna
> versate manu, versate diurna.

impudici vero poetae, superstitiosaeque nonnullae artes procul sint omnes a clerico. Opera vero atque industria Episcopi haec omnia recte praestabit, si unumquemque noverit clericorum, saepiusque ad se accersiri iusserit; percunctandoque tentaverit quantum unusquisque proficiat. quod si quis non profecerit repugnante natura, saltem ne labatur in peius, procurabit: sicque iuniores erudiet ut singulis pro ratione profectus conferat etiam dignitates. senes vero an officio suo desint inquiret, eosque mulctabit, qui deerunt. qui vero bene se gesserint, laudabit, premioque afficiet si occasio dabitur.

---

[33] V 42r and O 24v have "plerisque Pontificum ac clericorum."

were trained right from their youth in culture and upright morals. He will take care that the younger men are not trained in various humanist studies and the like, except to a sufficient degree, but in Christian discipline, in theology, I say, *not that of a contentious and obstinate sort, if I may say so, which puffs up the soul with a certain vanity and does more harm than good, but the teachings of the ancient theologians,* as well as in the pontifical law that befits that theology. *For that contentious law, which deals with the rights and legal quarrels of priests, was clearly contrived by the many flatterers of the clergy (I am speaking freely as the subject demands), and allows that any deed can seem to be done legally—I will say no more. I really think that little weight should be given to it; indeed, in those places where the jurists of our time disagree with the early theologians, it should be totally ignored.*[48] Still the study of the sacred scripture, which should have the last word in any and all the studies of clerics, should take precedence over everything else. They should always have these books in their hands, so we may say about our sacred writers what Flaccus says about the Greek writers,

> O you priests, keep in your hands the sacred books
> by night, keep them by day.[49]

May all the lewd poets and the many superstitious arts be far from a clergyman. The bishop's effort and work will perfectly achieve all these things if he shall have known each of his clergy and will have ordered them to come to see him frequently. By questioning [them] he will test how much progress each of them has made. If somebody shall not have made progress because his nature is in rebellion, he will at least keep him from slipping down lower. This way he will teach the younger men how he also confers honors on individuals as measured by their progress. He will inquire if the older men are falling short of their duty and will punish those who have fallen short. He will praise those who have conducted themselves well, and he

---

[48] The deletion of this passage in the 1579 and 1589 Venetian editions is by far the most important change made by the censors. The typesetters spaced out the page so that its end coincided with that of the Paris edition—this seems not so much designed to mislead readers as to make typesetting easier for the rest of the work.

[49] Horace, *Ars poetica*, verse 269. Contarini slightly modifies the text to sharpen his point.

Diligentissime quoque horum iura tuebitur, ne sacrorum ministri habeantur ludibrio, sed sustinere queant decus et maiestatem sacerdotalis dignitatis. maiori tamen sedulitate utatur opus est, in his sacerdotibus curandis, quibus alios regendi cura commissa est; a quibus poenitentiae Sacramento veluti pharmaco, populi delicta ablui purgarique solent, *qui iuniores*[34] *quidam Episcopi appellari possunt.*

Ac non tantum in urbe hoc procurabit, sed in oppidis villisque: licet non ea doctrina, neque ea studiorum ratio, quae ab urbano requiritur a rustico quoque sacerdote requirenda sit. non tamen rudem omnino literarum rusticum sacerdotem esse vellem,[35] sed tantam in literis profecisse, quantum sit satis ad erudiendos rusticos homines in his, quae necesse est quemlibet Christianum nosse: praecipue tamen bonos mores atque integram vitam ab his requiri debere admoneo.[36] Nihil enim magis noxium Christiano gregi quam improbus atque inhonestus sacerdos. Hactenus de clericis nulli certo ordine obstrictis. At illi qui sub aliquo ordine familiave merent, ex praerogativa quadam Romani Pontificis, Episcopi curae solent non subesse, verum duces seorsum habent, sub quibus militent. Non tamen propterea Episcopo cessandum duco, quin et hortetur praesides coenobiorum, ut monasteria in religione contineant, et si quis eorum forte facinus quodpiam perpetraverit, quod cedere queat in aliorum detrimentum, pro virili procuret, ut ex urbe pellatur suae fidei commissa, si alia ratione non dabitur manantem pestem coercere. Atque haec quidem privata quaedam officia sunt, quibus erga clerum utendum est.

Nunc vero erga universum populum communia quaedam [424] officia persequamur. Diebus solennibus, quorum plerique sunt anniversarii, officium Episcopi est, ut missarum solemnia sacra coram universo populo celebret, vesperis quoque adsit choris princeps, vestibus sacris indutus oleum chrismatis ipse conficiat, atque caerimonias alias sibi conficiendas potius quam aliis mandandas existimet. nam, ut inquit Paulus, qui Episcopatum

---

[34] V 43r and O 25r have "minores."

[35] In V 43r and O 25r this clause reads, "nollem tamen omnino rudem literarum esse quamvis rusticum sacerdotem."

[36] V 43v and O 25r have, "atque incontaminatam vitam ab his requirat."

will reward them if an opportunity arises. He will guard with great care their rights so that the ministers of the sacred rites may not be held in contempt but can rather uphold the honor and majesty of priestly dignity. He needs to use greater diligence in correcting those priests to whom the care of directing others has been entrusted. Through them the sins of the people are usually cleansed and washed away by the sacrament of penance as if by a medicine; *these men can be called junior bishops.*

He will undertake this not only in the city but also in the towns and villages, although the learning and the program of studies which is required of the urban priest should not also be expected of the country priest. Still I would not want the country priest to be completely uncultivated in letters; [I would want him] to have made as much progress in letters as is enough to teach the country folk about the things that every Christian needs to know. Still, I urge that from these [priests] good morals and a wholesome life are the main expectations. For nothing is more offensive to a Christian flock than an immoral and dishonorable priest. So far [our discussion has been] about clerics who are not bound to a specific order. But [priests] who serve in some order or congregation are not usually under the care of a bishop through some prerogative of the Roman Pontiff; they have their own separate leaders under whom they do battle. Still I do not think that the bishop should be stopped thereby from encouraging the superiors of convents to preserve their monasteries in religious behavior, and if one of their men should perchance have committed any crime which could lead to the harm of others, let [the bishop] do his utmost that he be driven out of the city entrusted to [the bishop's] care if he is not given another way to stem the spreading disease. These are certain private duties which should be employed regarding a clergy man.

Now let us go on to certain duties which are common to the whole people. It is the bishop's duty on solemn feasts, most of which are annual festivals, to celebrate a solemn mass before all the people; let him also preside over the choir at vespers; clothed in the sacred vestments let him personally consecrate the oil of chrism, and let him be of the opinion that he himself should perform the other ceremonies rather than delegate them to others. For as Paul says, "the person

desiderat, opus desiderat non quietam ac desidem vitam. illud etiam
non ab re erit, ut moneam nostrae tempestatis Episcopos, ne penitus
omittant vetustissimum morem a patribus nostris diligentissime
servatum, solebant illi celebres viri diebus festis, atque interdum
quotide inter missarum sacra orationem habere ad universum
populum, qua et erudiebant ignaros Christianarum rerum, et ad bene
vivendum mirifice universos hortabantur. extant non solum
Episcoporum, sed etiam summorum Pontificum quamplurimae
excellentissimaeque orationes ad populum habitae; quod munus
religiosi nostris temporibus usurparunt ob laguorem ac segnitiem
Episcoporum, cum tamen hoc onus, immo potius honor erudiendi
populi maxime proprium Episcoporum sit. vellem si non omnino,
aliquo saltem pacto morem hunc instaurari, ac in pristinum restitui
ab eo praeside, quem erudimus. nam festis quibusque diebus, et qui
aliqua insigni celebritate aguntur, sermonem ei habendum censerem,
quo vel Evangelium declararetur, vel aliqua ex sacris literis aut ex
morali philosophia in medium adducerentur: si minus coram universo
populo, saltem praesente atque audiente clero, nam per clerum ad
omnes quoque eam orationem manaturam verisimile est. nequaquam,
ut reor, huic officio bonus Episcopus deerit, nisi penitus se ineptum
esse senserit ad id praestandum; de qua re potius aliorum quam suo
iudicio credat.

Proximum huic officium est, ut non monitu atque hortatione
duntaxat, sed decretis legumque sanctione, universum populum in
recto religionis proposito contineat: Hoc vero facillime assequetur, si
duo contraria inter se vitia, quae plerunque in coetu hominum
pullulare solent, medio quodam tenore devitet. Horum alterum
irreligiositatem seu impietatem nominabimus, alterum vero
superstitionem: prius vitium oritur plerunque ex quibusdam
disciplinis et artibus religioni adversantibus, quae sapientiae nomen
praeseferunt, cum tamen verae sapientiae adversentur. Huiusmodi
autem artes sunt, nonnullae scientiae divinandi, ut Magia et
Astrologia, quas omnes sub idolatriae genere contineri compertum
esse potest omnibus, qui norint per has artes astris seu daemonibus
id ascribi, quod tantum divinae naturae est proprium: nec minus

who aspires to the office of bishop"[50] desires a task, not a quiet and idle life. It will not be beside the point if I admonish the bishops of our day against completely omitting the very ancient practice preserved most carefully by our fathers: those illustrious men were wont on feast days, and sometimes daily, during the sacred rites of mass to give a sermon to the whole people in which they taught those ignorant of Christian doctrine and wonderfully encouraged all to a good life. There are extant many superb sermons given to the people not only by bishops but also by the supreme pontiffs. This task the religious in our times have usurped because of the lethargy and laziness of the bishops; still this work, rather this honor, of teaching the people is above all the prerogative of bishops. I would like to see this custom restored, if not completely, at least to some degree and returned to its original form by the bishop whom we are teaching. For I feel that he should give a sermon on all feast days and on days which entail some special celebration. He should explain the Gospel or bring forward for discussion something from the sacred scriptures or from moral philosophy, if not before the whole people, at least with the clergy present and listening, for through the clergy that sermon will also very likely flow out to everybody. To my way of thinking, the good bishop will in no wise shirk this duty unless he feels himself totally incapable of doing it. On this point he should trust the judgment of others more than his own.

His duty next after this one is that he keep the whole people on the right path of religion not only by admonishment and encouragement but also by decrees and the sanction of laws. He will achieve this most easily if he avoids by a certain middle road two vices which are opposites of each other and which tend to sprout forth in most groups of men. We shall call one of these irreligiosity or impiety and the other superstition. The first vice generally arises from certain studies or arts opposed to religion; they lay claim to the name of wisdom but are nonetheless opposed to true wisdom. These kinds of arts are the various sciences of divination, such as magic and astrology. All of them can be recognized as a form of idolatry by all who know that what is proper to the divine nature alone is ascribed through these arts to the stars or to demons. No less does a

---

[50] 1 Tim 3:1.

quoddam philosophandi genus, quod nostra tempestate in gymnasiis inolevit a religione discrepat, penitusque dissentit, deviosque ducit ignaros adolescentes, qui cum nihil sciant, ex nescio quibusdam figmentis magnam de se opinionem scientiae nanciscuntur: adeo ut prae se alios nihili faciant, ignarosque rerum naturae putent merumque vulgus nuncupent. has omnes pernitiosissimas artes Episcopus pro virili procul pellat a suo grege: sanciatque omnes huiusmodi artes tanquam religioni adversantes, ab omnibus fugiendas esse atque reiiciendas; idque ut fiat, et sanctionibus, ut dixi, et sermonibus hortationibusque [425] sedulo curet. Huc pertinet illa diligentia, quam summam adhibere debet Episcopus, ne haeresis serpat, neque libri Haereticorum latenter in suam dioecesim importentur. Nulla enim capitalior pestis, nec quae facilius atheismo fenestram patefaciat quam haeresis est, quae fundamenta fidei cum tollat, etiam omnem Reipublicae statum subito evertit.[37]

Alterum vero peccatum huic contrarium est superstitio, quae excessus quidam religionis est, sicuti superius vitium defectus est quidam. omnis itaque superstitio diligenter tollatur: ita ut cum vel sancti, qui vitam agunt in coelis invocantur, vel cum eorum reliquas veneramur: vel cum imagines Domini et beatissimae virginis, aliorumve in Ecclesiis pinguntur, omnia honestissime ordinateque fiant, illamque plebem ad Dei unius cultum quemadmodum decet, quasi per gradus manu ducant. Prudenti autem Episcopo, et Ecclesiastico facile fuerit, si quis in his rebus abusus irrepsit, sensim abolere: ne si inconsiderate, sive praecipites feramur, ipsum iam Dei cultum, fidemque Sacramentorum, ordinem quoque Hierarchicum Ecclesiae, ut heretici fecerunt, tollamus. Doceatur itaque saepe populus in omnibus et super omnia Deum amandum atque colendum

---

[37] As Gigliola Fragnito points out in *Gasparo Contarini*, p. 187, that the last two sentences seem to be an interpolation by the person charged with preparing the Paris edition; heretical books were not a threat in 1517. At this point the Paris edition suppresses a long passage condemning popular religious superstitions found in V 45v-48v and O 26v-27r. An appendix of this work prints and translates the missing passage.

certain type of philosophy, which in our time has flourished in the schools, deviate and completely disagree with religion and lead astray ignorant adolescents who, since they know nothing, light upon a high opinion of their own knowledge from I know not what illusions, so much so that in comparison with themselves they account others as worthless and think them ignorant of the nature of things and deride them as mere rabble.[51] Let the bishop with his whole strength drive all these deadly arts far from his flock. Let him forbid under punishment all these kinds of arts, which everybody should flee and reject, as hostile to religion. As I said, to bring this about let him zealously bring to bear punishments, sermons, and exhortations. To this applies that diligence which the bishop should employ in greatest measure lest heresy creep in or the books of heretics be secretly imported into his diocese. There is no more deadly disease nor one that more easily opens the window to atheism than heresy, which, because it destroys the foundations of faith, also quickly subverts the whole basis of the state.

Opposite to this is the other sin of superstition, which is in a sense too much religion, just as the previous vice was in a way too little. Therefore all superstition must be diligently destroyed: thus when the saints, who live in heaven, are invoked or when we venerate their relics or when the images of the Lord and the Blessed Virgin or of others are depicted in churches, everything should be done in a respectful and orderly way and should lead the common people by the hand as if step by step to the worship of the one God, as is fitting. It will be easy for the wise bishop or churchman to abolish gradually any abuse in these matters that creeps in; otherwise we may be carried along in a thoughtless, headlong way and destroy the worship of God itself, faith in the sacraments, and the hierarchical order of the Church too, as the heretics have done. Therefore let the people be often taught that God is to be loved and worshipped in all and above

---

[51] Here Contarini was almost certainly thinking about his former fellow students at the University of Padua who were captivated by the Averroism of some professors. With these professors in mind, the Fifth Lateran Council in 1513 condemned the teaching that the human soul was mortal or that all persons shared the same soul. In the same year that Contarini wrote his *De officio episcopi* he also wrote a tract defending the immortality of the soul; it was published in February 1518 together with a reply by Pietro Pomponazzi, Contarini's teacher and the greatest of the Paduan Aristotelians. Contarini later incorporated the tract in his *De Immortalitate animae*. On the controversy with Pomponazzi, see Gleason, 76-82.

esse, omnia autem propter Deum, sine quo nihil est factum; sanctique ipsi nihil essent. ita omnis actio, cogitatioque ab ipso proficiscatur, et ·in ipsum denique, ut alpha et omega, referatur. si ad sanctos confugiant, noscant cur id faciant, caeteraque, quae a synodis sapientissime decreta sunt, et exposita. quod si quis aut ob avaritiam, aut ob aliam causam reliquiis, aut imaginibus sacris abuteretur, protinus tales pestes ab Ecclesia Dei arceantur, gravique mulcta afficiantur, ne hisce monstris Christiana puritas inquinetur. *Superstitionis* {Suspitionis} errore impietatisque scelere vitatis, facile in recta religione populus poterit contineri. procuret tamen, ut quilibet suis saltem temporibus poenitentiae et Eucharistiae Sacramenta frequentet; idque diligenter sciscitetur ab antistitibus, qui urbis regionibus ac vicis praesunt.[38]

Cui officio si quis deerit, primum nitatur ad se accersitum suasionibus lenique increpatione ad rectum pietatis iter, ad munus revocare. quod si pertinaci mente aliquem sceleri cuipiam adstrictum corrigi nolle senserit, tunc mulctis notisque Ecclesiasticis mulctatum infamem caeteris reddat, ne contagione pestis illius caeteri quoque inficiantur. Curet praeterea adolescentium institutionem, ac pro virili non permittat statim ab ineunte aetate puerorum animos corrumpi poetarum, caeterorumque huiusmodi auctorum lasciviis: quas si a teneris annis imbiberint; impossibile prope erit, ut in maturori aetate meliorem frugem revocentur. qua in re nostris temporibus, ut in primo libro diximus, magnopere peccatur. praeclare enim Aristoteles in Ethicis non parum, inquit, sed totum differt quomodo quis ab adolescentia assuescat. quamobrem divinus quoque Plato in libris de Republica iure optimo execrari Poetas videtur, et ab ea civitate pellere, quam optimam ipse instituit. Non tamen propterea quempiam suspicari velim nos

---

[38] Only the first and last sentences of this paragraph are found in the two manuscripts examined. The rest of the paragraph was clearly added by the Paris editor as a substitute for the much longer section that he suppressed.

all, but all other things [are to be loved] because of the God. Without Him nothing has been made and the saints themselves would be nothing. Thus let all action and thought proceed from Him and return to Him in the end, as the Alpha and Omega. If [the people] seek refuge in the saints, let them know why they do so, together with an explanation of the other articles which the councils have most wisely decreed and explained. If somebody abuses relics or sacred images out of greed or for some other reason, let such plagues be immediately driven from God's church and undergo severe punishment lest Christian purity be polluted with these horrors. After the error of *superstition* {imperfect notions} and the crime of impiety have been avoided, the people will easily be held together in right religion. Still he should insure that everybody make use of the sacraments of penance and the eucharist at least at their [proper] times; the leading priests who have charge over the urban districts and the villages should look into this carefully.

If somebody shall have fallen short of his office, first let [the bishop] summon him to himself and try to recall him to the right path of piety and duty by advice and gentle admonition. But if he feels that somebody with a stubborn mindset or an addiction to some sin does not want to be reformed, then let [the bishop] disgrace him before others, after punishing him with ecclesiastical punishments and censures lest other people too be infected by the contagion of that plague. In addition let him care for the education of young people, and let him do his utmost not to permit the souls of boys at the onset of manhood to be immediately corrupted by the licentiousness of the poets and other writers of that sort.[52] If they shall have drunk in [licentiousness] in their tender years, it will be almost impossible to recall them to better fare at a more mature age. On this point our times have sinned greatly, as we said in the first book. Aristotle in the *Ethics* says not a few excellent things, but he completely sidesteps how one picks up habits from his youth.[53] Wherefore the divine Plato in the books of his *Republic* also seems to denounce poets with full justice and cast them out of that state which he sets up as an ideal.[54] Still I would not want anybody to suspect on that account

---

[52] Ovid, Catullus, and Boccaccio were obvious targets.
[53] Aristotle, *Nicomachean Ethics*, II, 1 (1103b 22-25).
[54] Plato, *Republic*, III, 401b.

eodem ordine Poetas omnes habere, neque intelligere, *divinum* {non nunquam superiorem} quendam afflatum Poetis inesse: non adeo rudes sumus adeoque tardo ingenio, ut id non sentiamus.

Verum longe praeferendam censemus animi integritatem, ac pudicitiam [426] voluptati illi, ac titillationi, quae ex lectione poetarum huiusmodi capi solet. paulatim nanque tabes dulci cantu perfusa, divinoque poetae spiritu condita repit in animum, penitusque inhaeret: ut postmodum vix unquam ablui queat. ab huiusmodi poetarum studiis abstinere debent adolescentes. si quis vero, ut apud latinos Virgilius,[39] vel componendis moribus studet, quod optimum est, vel bella tempestatesque canit, eum non esse legendum non pronuntio, immo laudo, si quis ita legit, ut ab eo non solum delectetur, sed etiam iuvetur.[40] Sed interim si fieri posset, ut cum profanis[41] auctoribus simul aliqua Christiana lectio pueris discenda proponeretur, mirum quam bene id fieret. Nam, ut verum fateamur, turpissimum est Christi pietatem profitentibus, Romanorum gesta, caerimoniasque, atque auguria nosse, Christianam vero religionem penitus ignorare. utinam nostro Episcopo auctore talis inolesceret consuetudo, ut pueri continuo ab infantia (ut ita dicam) Christianis lectionibus assuescerent. Sunt enim etiam apud nos auctores latini satis multi, ne fortasse aliquis vereatur, ne eloquentia latina studiis sacrarum literarum corrumpatur. sed iam satis persecuti videmur pro nostri operis modo Episcopi officia circa virorum gubernationem impendenda: quae ad eorum institutionem atque in Christiana pietate profectum pertinere videatur.

Sequitur,[42] ut pauca quaedam dicamus, quae curare Episcopus debeat circa mulierum vitam. hae quoniam virorum imperio suditae sunt, generali quadam ratione gubernari debent. singula vero eorum

---

[39] V 49v and O 28v add "et Flaccus," that is, Horace.

[40] V49v and O 28v have simply "... canit, eius studium non reprehendo." The rest of the sentence is the editor's interpolation.

[41] V 49v and O 28v have "gentilibus."

[42] V 50r and O 28v have "Nunc tempus poscere videtur".

that we lump all the poets in the same category and do not understand that there is a certain *divine* {sometimes a higher} inspiration in the poets, for we are not so uncouth or of such backward intelligence that we are unaware of that.

But we regard the soul's integrity and modesty far above the pleasure and amusement which is usually gained from reading poets of that sort. For gradually decay, steeped in the sweet song and made flavorful by the divine spirit of the poet, creeps into the soul and becomes wholly ingrained so that after a short time it can hardly ever be washed out. Young people should stay away from studying these sorts of poets. If somebody, for example Virgil among the Latin [authors], works toward restoring morals, which is excellent, or singing about storms and wars, I do not claim that he should not be read; indeed I praise anybody who reads [him] in such a way that he not only draws delight from him but also finds help. But if it is meanwhile possible to propose that children study some Christian reading together with the pagan authors, how wonderful it would be![55] For to tell the truth, it is shameful how those who profess devotion to Christ know the deeds, ceremonies, and auguries of the Romans but are utterly ignorant about the Christian religion. Would that the custom would grow, under the guidance of our bishop, that boys right from their infancy (if I may say so) became accustomed to Christian literature. For there are among us quite enough Latin writers, lest perhaps somebody may be fearful of his Latin eloquence being corrupted by studying sacred letters. But by now we seem, given the scope of our work, to have traced out the duties of the bishop employed in governing men. This seems to be related to their education and progress in Christian piety.

We have next to say a few things about how the bishop should care for women's lives. Since they are subject to the control of men, they should be governed by a certain general principle. Their individual ac-

---

[55] The use of even "good" pagan authors such as Virgil, Horace, and Cicero was attacked by some leaders of Catholic reformation. Contarini's friends Tommaso Giustiniani and Vincenzo Querini attacked their use in their famous reform *Libellus* to Leo X, Fragnito, "Cultura umanistica," 171. The Jesuits at Milan clashed with St. Carlo Borromeo in 1568 because they wanted to keep such authors in their curriculum while the Cardinal, like Giustiani and Querini, wanted to replace pagan poets with Prudentius and Christian writers: Flavio Rurale, *I Gesuiti a Milano. Religione e Politica nel secondo Cinquecento* (Rome: Bulzoni Editore, 1992) 119.

gesta maribus, quibus parent, moderanda linquantur. atque hoc de
laicis mulieribus dictum esse intelligatur.[43] eas vero, quae Deo
virginitatem vovere, atque in coenobiis degunt; non modo communi
quadam ratione ut alias, Episcopus tueri, ac regere debet; verum
omnem operam adhibere, ne ignoret, vel minimam earum culpam.
nam periculosum admodum est in lubrico eo sexu, parum etiam
deflexisse de via. Nisi enim principiis obstiteris, frustra postmodum
retinacula contrahas, cum in praeceps delatae iam retineri non possunt,
quin omnino ruant.[44] quae res quanto dedecori sit Christianae
religioni, in quantam civitatis ignonimiam cedat, satis explicari non
potest. Nequeo hoc loco non summopere indignari, celebres nonnullas
ac principes Christianorum urbes adeo hac peste coinquinatas esse,
ut pleraque monasteria virginum olim Deo dicata lupanarium vicem
praebeant. quo quid turpius, quid sceleratius excogitari potest? cur
tandem ludibrio sanctissimam Christianam religionem obnoxiam haec
culpa non facit apud eos omnes, qui alieni a Christi grege, aut
iudaicam, aut Maumeticam, aut haereticam[45] perfidiam profitentur?
quamobrem in primis Episcopi officium reor providere, ne quod
huiusmodi scelus in ea, cui praeest, civitate contingat diligenterque
scrutetur commercia, ac consuetudines monacharum: ut principiis
obstare possit. Si quando vero (quod avertat Deus) contractam alicubi
hanc tabem senserit, ad vivum usque resecet; imploret opem a principe
civitatis, obsecret, obtestetur, imperet Dei iussu, ne hanc iniuriam
patiatur fieri divino nomini: nullo tandem in munere se magis
ardentem praebeat. Non tamen propterea laudaverim, ut Episcopus,
aut quivis Episcopi minister familiaritate, ac frequenti [427] monacharum consuetudine utatur. Nam praeterquam quod periculosa est ea
familiaritas, certe plerunque culpae suspicionem praebet. qua maxime

---

[43] In V 50r and O 28v this sentence reads "quod de prophanis mulieribus
dictum sit."

[44] V 50v and O 29r read: "sed in praeceps delatae ad summum impudicitatae
ruent."

[45] V 51r and O 29r lack "aut haereticam."

tions may be left to the directions of the males to whom they are obedient. This should be understood as said about lay women. But the bishop should guard and direct those who vow virginity to God and live in convents not merely on the same common basis as other women, but he should bend every effort so as not to be ignorant of even their smallest fault. For it is very dangerous for the weaker sex to swerve even a little from the path. For if you have not been resolute in the first instances, you later tighten the reins in vain, since women who have fallen headlong can no longer be restrained from plunging to complete destruction. How much dishonor that would bring to the Christian religion and how much shame would result for the city defy full description. I cannot at this juncture keep from becoming extremely angry because this plague has so befouled some major Christian cities that very many convents of virgins once dedicated to God are converted into brothels.[56] How could anything more foul, more criminal be imagined? Finally, why does not this sin make the most holy Christian religion shameful among all those who are outside the Christian flock or who profess either Jewish, or Moslem, or heretical falsehood? I therefore think the bishop has a major responsibility to see to it that no crime of this sort occurs in the city over which he presides and that he carefully scrutinize the dealings and acquaintanceships of the nuns so that he can prevent this from the outset. If sometime he shall have felt that this corruption had been contracted anywhere (may God avert it!), he will amputate right to the quick. Let him implore, beseech, beg and demand by the mandate of God help from the prince of the city lest this insult to the divine name be allowed to exist.[57] Lastly, let there be no duty about which he shows himself more zealous. But I would not on that account praise the bishop or any of the bishop's staff for cultivating familiarity or frequent dealings with nuns. Aside from the fact that such familiarity is dangerous, it gives much rise to suspicion of sin. He, whose

---

[56] On the extreme breakdown of sexual morality in some Venetian convents during Contarini's time, see Guido Ruggiero, *The Boundaries of Eros: Sex Crime and Sexuality in Renaissance Venice* (New York: Oxford University Press, 1985) 77-84.

[57] For an overview of Italian convents for women and their reform see Gabriella Zarri, "Monasteri femminili e città (secoli XV-XVIII)," in *Storia d'Italia, Annali 9: La chiesa e il potere politico dal medioevo all'età contemporanea*, edited by Giorgio Chittolini and Giovanni Miccoli, (Turin: Einaudi, 1986) 357-429; on the need for cooperation of bishops and civil authorities in Venetian territory, 381-384.

carendum est illi, cuius vita veluti exemplar caeteris proposita esse debet. illud adeo dicere ausim, peiorem fere esse in Episcopo suspicionem innoxiam, quam latentem culpam.

Nunc quando de monachis mulieribus dictum est, restat ut pauca quaedam de laicis[46] quoque dicamus. Hae cum virorum imperio sint subiectae: generali tantum ac communi quadam ratione ab Episcopo curari debent. praetereo quaedam superius de viris praecepta, quae ad mulieres quoque pertinent, ut quotannis scilicet poenitentiae, et Eucharistiae Sacramenta frequentent, huiusmodi alia nonnulla dicam quaedam solum, quae ipsarum tantum sunt, nequaquam vero spectant ad viros. primum nitendum pro viribus est, ut decenti, pudico moderatoque cultu corporis utantur, iuxta regulam Apostoli Pauli; Non in tortis crinibus et cetera. impudicus enim immodicusque mulierum ornatus religioni Christianae adversatur, et reipublicae bono. Nam primum eius, quae eo utitur cultu, mores corrumpit, dum enim se suamque pulchritudinem, atque ornatum admiratur et diligit, tum sui, tum Dei obliviscitur, seque aliis mulieribus digniorem excellentioremque facit. menteque turgida nil non superbum, nil non iniurium aliis sapit. haec prima est labes, primaque mentis corruptio: qua infecta facile ad impudicitiam prolabitur. Nec minus obest mulierum immodicus atque impudicus ornatus iuvenibus viris, qui facilius immoderati cultus muliebris illecebris ad libidines alliciuntur. hinc in sanctissimis templis amores exercent oculis atque nutibus, passimque inter se de amoribus sermones conferunt.[47] obiter hoc in loco, quando in huius rei mentionem incidimus, admonendus nobis Episcopus est, ut suasionibus, increpationibus, sanctionibusque illud conficiat: ne Dei immortalis templis[48] pro areis et foro cives utantur, per ea deambulando, et inter se de mercatura, de bellis, plerunque vero de amoribus disserendo, sed religiose sancteque in illis versentur.

Nunc revertamur ad mulierum ornatum, quem quidem religionis primum adversari institutis affirmamus, si nimis diffluat, deinde etiam reipublicae bono tantum nocere, ut nihil supra.[49] dum enim magni

---

[46] V 51v and O 29r have "prophanis."

[47] V 52r and O 29v read: "hinc in deorum templis nutibus amores exercent inter se de amoribus sermones crebro conferunt."

[48] V 52r and O 29v have have "deorum templis" for "Dei immortalis templis."

[49] In V 52r and O 29v the sentence reads: "Nunc revertamur ad mulierum ornatum, quae si immodicus fuerit, religionis institutis primum ostendimus adversari, nec minus reipublicae bono nocere."

life should be held up as a model to others, should be extremely careful on this point. I would have even dared to say that a groundless suspicion about a bishop is almost worse than a hidden sin.

Now that women religious have been discussed, it remains that we should say a few things about lay women. Since they are subject to the control of their husbands, they should be under the care of the bishop only in a general and ordinary way. I pass over some of the precepts [given] above for men which also apply to women, namely that they frequent the sacraments of penance and the eucharist annually. I will say something in this regard about the things which belong exclusively to women and have no relevance to men. First, every effort should be bent that they take a decent, modest, and restrained care of their bodies, in accord with the rule of the Apostle Paul, "Not with braided hair" and so forth.[58] Shameless and immodest dressing up by women is opposed to the Christian religion and the good of the state. For it first corrupts the morals of the woman who uses such care, for while she admires and loves herself and her beauty, she then forgets about both herself and God and makes herself more worthy and more excellent than other women. With mind puffed up, she savors nothing that is not prideful and harmful to others. This is the first stain and the first corruption of the mind— infected with this, she easily slides into unchastity. Shameless and immodest dressing up by women is no less harmful to young men, who are more easily stirred to passionate desires by the allurement of immodest feminine adornment. Hence they do their romancing with eyes and nods in the most holy churches and generally discuss their love affairs with one another. Incidentally on this point: while we interrupt to mention this business, we should warn the bishop that by urging, beseeching and by regulations he should bring it about that the citizens not use the churches of the immortal God as a playground or public square, walking around them, discussing among themselves business deals, wars but especially love affairs, but in them they should conduct themselves in a religious and holy way.

Now let us go back to women's attire, which we assert is first opposed to the practices of religion if it is overdone, and secondly it also does more harm to the state than anything else [mentioned]

---

[58] 1 Tim 2:9: "Women should adorn themselves modestly and sensibly in seemly apparel, not with braided hair or gold or pearls or costly attire but by good deeds."

sumptus in ornatum mulierum a viris fiunt, alteraque alteram superare
contendit; magna fit civium rei domesticae totiusque tandem civitatis opum iactura. cohibendus ergo continendusque erit iuxta praecepta
Apostoli mulierum cultus. illud quoque praecipiendum reor, curare
Episcopum debere, ne impudicis spectaculis mulieres intersint.
Corrumpunt mores bonos, mentisque integritatem labefactant turpia
spectacula, quaeque in eis obscoena dicuntur, atque aguntur.[50] Hoc
idem in pueris providendum erit. priscis quidem temporibus
huiusmodi spectaculis ac fabulis, quae publice recitantur, magnam
operam dabant, maximisque sumptibus publice instructa erant
theatra, in quibus populus ad prophana ea, et impudica spectacula
conveniebat. quod veteres satyrici poetae increpant vehementer.
postmodum vero, cum Christiana veritas illuxit, patrum nostrorum
institutis sublata fuere. nostra vero tempestate in plerasque Italiae
civitates obrepsit hic morbus, qui a praeside Christiano tollendus
penitus esset, si fieri posset; sin minus, saltem hac ratione cohibendus,
ut pueri, ac mulieres [428] ab huiusmodi spectaculis abstinerent.

Caeterum quoniam nuptae mulieres, ac pueri, qui parentes habent
superstites, minus obnoxii iniuriae sunt, vivendique praeceptores
parentes habent, ac maritos: iccirco universali quadam ratione ab
Episcopo sunt instituendi, eisque non peculiari quodam modo, sed
communi subsidium ferendum est. At pupilli, et viduae quae expositae
sunt iniuriae, neque proprios praeceptores habent, qui eos recte
instituere valeant, praecipua quadam ope tuendi sunt. Episcopus enim
communis quidam est pater totius civitatis, a quo illi, qui magis indi-
gent, magis item sublevandi atque adiuvandi sunt. Hinc est quod
sacris literis praecipue commendantur hi, qui pupillum et viduam
fovent, ab eisque propulsant iniuriam. quamobrem his utrisque
Christianum praesidem decet maiore animi cura atque studio acriore
opem ferre, ad eosque recte instituendos omnem diligentiam adhibere.
satis arbitror hucusque a nobis explicata sunt officia Episcopi: quae
civitati, cui praeest, instituendae atque in Christiana pietate
continendae accommodata videntur: eoque processimus ordine, quem
charitatis iura praescribunt.

---

[50] V 52v and O 30r have only "turpia spectacula obscoenaque in eis dicta."

above. For while men go to great expense in dressing up women, and one woman struggles to outdo another, there is an enormous waste of the citizens' domestic property and ultimately of the whole city's wealth. Therefore feminine ornamentations should be checked and restricted in accord with the Apostle's precepts.[59] I think that the bishop should take care that it be commanded that women are not to attend shameful theater performances. Disgraceful performances corrupt good morals and undermine mental integrity, for in them obscene acts are discussed and performed. It will be good to apply this same [restriction] to boys. In ancient times they used to lavish great effort on these sorts of spectacles and on the stories that were recited in public; theaters were constructed for the public at enormous expense; in them the people gathered for these profane and indecent performances. The ancient satirical poets bitterly criticized this. Indeed later when the Christian light shined forth, they were destroyed at the instigation of our fathers. But in our time, this disease has crept into most Italian cities, which a Christian governor should totally abolish if it is possible; but if not, at least it should be restricted by this principle: that boys and women stay away from such spectacles.

For the rest, since married women and boys who have living parents are less liable to damage and have parents and husbands to teach them how to live, therefore the bishop should educate them in a certain general way, and they should be given help in a common rather than in an individualized way. But orphans and widows, who are exposed to damage and do not have their own teachers who can bring them up right, should be protected by some special help. For the bishop is the common father of the whole city who should give greater encouragement and help those who have the greater need. This is why those are especially praised in the sacred writings who help the orphan and widow and drive injustice away from them.[60] Therefore it befits the Christian leader to bring both of these help with greater care of soul and more eager zeal and to employ all diligence to bring them up right. I think that so far we have sufficiently described the bishop's duties; these seem well adapted to training and maintaining in Christian piety the city over which he presides. From here we are proceeding in the order prescribed by the rights of charity.

[59] Ibid.
[60] James 1:27.

Nunc pauca quaedam dicenda restant de officis, quae circa opes, ac reditus Episcopatus versantur. Eorum enim distributio ad Christiani praesidis charitatem iure optimo spectare videtur. Nam si huiusmodi opum erogatio in sacris literis, ac praesertim in Evangelio, prophanis viris praecipitur: qui nullo religionis privato iure sunt obstricti: quique in comparandis sibi opibus insudarunt: quanto magis censendum est fuisse hoc Episcopis praeceptum qui perfectissimum in Christiana religione ordinem profitentur: quibusque opes non sudore partae, sed testamentis legatae sunt, ut cultui divino et egenorum necessitatibus inservirent. qua de causa verius procuratores quidam, ac tutores bonorum, quae pauperibus legata sunt, quam alia quavis appellatione nuncupari debent. Non ignoro tam in theologorum libris, quam in sacris canonibus sancitum esse, qua regula uti Episcopum oporteat, in redituum Episcopatus dispensatione. Nos vero praecepta dabimus: quae servanda esse putamus Episcopo viro bono, non autem illi, qui tanquam in foro sibi cum Deo litigandum esse putet, nihil aliud agere velit, quam id, quod ei sacris sanctionibus iniunctum esse appareat, quodque sine scelere praeterire non posset. hoc (mihi crede) non est agere ex charitate, sed ex mulctae timore: qui si absit, neque illud facias, quod nunc facis. hi qui hoc pacto servari a se oportere Episcopi munera existimant, intra praescriptos quosdam terminos liberalitatis, ac munificentiae continentur.

At charitas terminum nescit, nullis finibus cohibetur. quamobrem cum illud in primis studeamus, ut Episcopus, quem instituimus, charitatis igne accensus nil non ex charitatis praecepto faciat: iccirco

There remains the need to say some things about the duties which are involved in the bishopric's wealth and income. Their distribution seems to belong on good legal grounds to the charity of the Christian leader. For if the sacred scriptures and especially the Gospel[61] require this [charitable] disposal of wealth from lay men who are bound by no private religious law and who have sweated in acquiring wealth for themselves, we should think that this command applies much more to bishops who lay claim to the highest order of perfection in the Christian religion.[62] Their wealth was not created by their sweat but was bequeathed to them in legacies so that it might serve for divine worship and the needs of the poor. For this reason they should more accurately be called procurators and protectors of the goods which were bequeathed to the poor; this is more apt than any other name. I am not unaware that in both the books of the theologians and in sacred canons a rule is laid down which the bishop ought to follow in dispensing the income of the bishopric.[63] But we will give precepts which we think should govern a bishop who is a good man, not a person who thinks that he should enter into litigation with God, as if in a lawcourt. He would not want to do anything except that which seems to be enjoined on him by sacred laws and which cannot be evaded without a shameful crime. To do this (believe me) is not to act out of charity but out of fear of punishment. If fear were gone, you would not do what you are doing now. Those who think that they should carry out the duties of the bishop on this basis are constrained within certain prescribed limits of generosity and gift giving.

But charity knows no limit and is restricted by no boundaries. Wherefore since we are mainly eager that the bishop whom we are instructing may be aflame with the fire of charity and do nothing except what charity commands, let him then not be constrained by

[61] Matt 22:17-21.

[62] Confer Thomas Aquinas, S.T., II-II, 184, 6-7. Contarini touches this same point in more detail in his prefatory letter to Lippomano.

[63] Aquinas, S.T., II-II, 185, 7, discusses the different obligations bishops have for helping the poor from their personal wealth, from ecclesiastical goods given for divine worship, and from those given to help the poor. Bishops sin mortally and are bound to restitution if they retain for themselves or expend on divine worship what has been given for the poor. When goods are not designated specifically for the poor, bishops may use their discretion.

nullis praeceptorum angustiis contineatur, sed omne quod ex victus parci ac modici sumptibus reliquum est, cum divino cultui, tum maxime egenorum necessitatibus impendat. turpissmum enim ac maxime nefarium reor, velle quempiam ex inopum peculio divitias sibi comparare, aut bona pauperum in supellectilem domus magnificam, in longum servorum ordinem; caeterosque huiusmodi sumptus profundere. de quibus, quoniam supra abunde satis a nobis est [429] dictum, cum de vita ac victu Episcopi loqueremur, nil in praesentia amplius puto dicendum esse, nisi ut dignitatem ordinis tueatur, superfluis impensis omnino reiectis, cumque nostra tempestate in sumptibus non necessariis magis peccetur, ille ad defectum potius tendere conetur. sic enim medium tenebit: in quo est virtus constituta: Divino igitur cultui primum id, quod necessarium est impendat, reliquum pauperibus eroget: quod si indigentia pauperum tanta esset, ut pro eorum vita tuenda oporteret aliquid demere de sumptibus quae in divino cultu de more fieri solent, censeo ego maxime secundum Christianam pietatem Episcopum facturum, si minus magnifice Deum coluerit in templis lapideis, ut resarciat, opemque ferat templis Dei non marmoreis et insensibilibus, sed viventibus, atque intelligentibus. Dei enim templum vos estis, inquit ille. quod si tanta necessitas eum non urgeat, Deum colat ea magnificentia, quae pro consuetudine, et urbis dignitate satis esse videatur. quod superest vero pauperibus eroget, sentiatque se procuratorem, ac tutorem potius pauperum esse, quam dominum: si quid autem adhuc supererit: ad ornatum templi id omne convertat.

pauperes vero non omnes eodem ordine habeat, sed potius opem ferat illis, qui ditioni suae subiecti sunt, quam externis. Nam ea videtur etiam mens fuisse illorum, qui bona sua legarunt Ecclesiae, cui praesidet, ut scilicet municipibus egenis potius quam externis ea erogentur. Petrus Barocius, de quo supra quoque a nobis facta est mentio, diligenter hoc servabat, malebatque Patavinis egenis opem ferre ex Episcopatus reditibus,

any narrow precepts but freely expend both on divine worship and especially on the needs of the poor all that is left over from the costs of a spare and modest lifestyle. I regard it very shameful and completely abominable for anybody to want to gather riches for himself from the pockets of the needy or to lavish the goods of the poor on magnificent home furniture, on a long rank of servants or other similar expenses. On these points I do not think I should say anything more now since we spoke in sufficient detail when discussing the bishop's lifestyle, except this: in order to keep up the dignity of his rank, he should lean rather toward a lack of spending and absolutely rule out all superfluous expenses since in our time the greater sin lies in unnecessary expenditures. Thus will he attain the mean in which virtue lies. Let him spend first on divine worship what is necessary, let him earmark the rest for the poor. But if the need of poor people is so great that to protect their lives it is necessary to subtract something from the normal expenses that customarily go for divine worship, I think the bishop will act very much in accord with Christian piety if he worships God less magnificently in temples of stone so that he may repair and bring help to God's temples which are not unfeeling marble but living, intelligent beings.[64] He says, "You are the temples of God."[65] But if such a great need does not press upon him, let him worship God with that magnificence which seems appropriate to the custom and dignity of the city. Let him earmark for the poor what is left over, to be sure; and let him consider himself the steward and protector of the poor rather than their lord; but if anything is still left over, let him turn it all over toward decorating the temple.

Let him not put all the poor in the same category but rather give help to those who are subject to his own jurisdiction rather than to outsiders. That also seems to have been the mind of those who bequeathed their goods to the church over which he presides, namely so that those [goods] might be earmarked for needy fellow citizens rather than for outsiders. Pietro Barozzi, about whom we also made mention above, carefully observed this norm and preferred to give help from the bishopric's income to needy Paduans than to his own

---

[64] This sentence seems close to statements in St. Ambrose's *De officiisministrorum*, II, ch. 28, nn. 137-38; Philip Schaff and Henry Wace, editors, *A Selected Library of Nicene and Post-Nicene Fathers of the Christian Church*, second series, vol. X, *St. Ambrose: Select Works and Letters* (reprinted, Grand Rapids: Eerdmans, 1955) 64.

quam Venetis consanguineis suis: quod diceret eam vim agrorum, villarumque testamentis a Patavinis civibus Episcopo legatam esse ea mente, ut quilibet coniectari facile potest; quo Patavinorum inopum necessitati ex his opibus subveniretur. inter inopes vero, bonos viros, bonique nominis mulieres aliis non probis semper praeferat. Hi etenim et Christo et nobis magis proximi sunt quam improbi, ac scelesti. scelestos tamen extrema indigentia oppressos non negligat. Deumque imitetur, qui ut sacrae perhibent literae, solem suum oriri aeque facit super iustos et iniustos, omnibus vero in hoc officio anteferendi sunt illi, quibus nobili genere ortis paupertas ignonimiae esse solet; neque mercenarias artes exercere sine calumnia queunt. his maxime tribuendum, neque expectandum, ut eleemosinas petant; verum his etiam non petentibus largiendum, et quandoque insciis. post hos alios curet pauperes. verum in hac largitione, et munificentia illud cavendum est, ne inertes nonnulli, quod frequenter accidit, liberalitate hac illecti se ocio dedant, segnemque ac tandem turpem vitam ducant.

attinet ad hoc officium etiam illud, uti Nosodochiorum sive hospitalium (utar enim novo vocabulo) curam habeat, quae Episcopo deberi videtur. Nam pleraque omnia hospitalia suos tutores, ac praesides habere solent, quibus haec cura praecipue debetur, quae et singula eorum visere aliquando Episcopi debebunt. Dubitabit hic aliquis, clam ne haec in pauperes munificentia, caeteraque virtutum officia praestari debeant, an potius aperte, ita ut omnes ea intelligant et [430] sciant. Arbitror ego in hac re, si praecepto

Venetian blood relatives. He used to say this power over the fields and villages was bequeathed to the bishop by the Paduan citizens in their wills with this understanding, as anybody can easily divine: so that the necessary expenses of poor Paduans might be underwritten by these riches. Let him always give preference among the poor to good men and women of good reputation over others who are not moral. For they are more neighbors to Christ and to us than are immoral and criminal persons. But let him not neglect criminals when they are crushed by extreme poverty. Let him imitate God, who makes his sun rise equally for the just and the unjust, as the sacred scriptures assert.[66] As regards this duty, those are to be preferred over everybody who, because they come from noble stock, usually find poverty shameful and cannot find employment in gainful jobs without losing face.[67] A generous allotment should be set aside for them; one should not wait for them to come begging for alms, but gifts should be made to them even without their asking, and sometimes without their even knowing it. Let him care for other poor people after them. But in this donation a certain magnificence should be avoided lest some lazy fellows, as happens often, enticed by this generosity give themselves over to leisure and lead a slothful and ultimately shameful life.

It is also part of this duty that he have that care which seems proper for a bishop as regards infirmaries or hospitals (let me use the new term). For most or all hospitals usually have their own protectors or superintendents, who have the main responsibility for this care. Bishops should sometimes look into each one of them. Here somebody will question whether this generosity toward the poor and the other duty-bound performance of the virtues should be done secretly or rather openly so that everybody may understand and know them. I judge that he will do very well on this point if he follows the

---

[65] 1 Cor 3:16.

[66] Matt 5:45.

[67] The preferential claim on alms that Contarini assigns to poor nobles was typical of contemporary Venetian society, or at least of the upper classes who gave the alms. See Brian Pullan, *Rich and Poor in Renaissance Venice: The Social Institutions of a Catholic State, to 1620* (Cambridge, MA: Harvard University Press, 1971) 228-31. Pullan makes explicit reference to Contarini's teaching on special treatment for the *poveri vergognosi* (p. 229) and notes that legislation for alms at Brescia "used phrases strongly redolent of Gasparo Contarini's admonitions to the bishop" (p. 278).

Augustini utatur, eum optime facturum. ille enim inquit oportere animi intentionem esse in occulto, bona vero opera, si inspiciantur et luceant, ut lux coram hominibus, prodesse. Non ergo ex his officiis laudem sibi Episcopus, aut ullam nominis celebritatem, (ambitiosum enim hoc esset) sed Dei laudem quaerat. hac enim ratione intentionem in occulto habebit, opera vero bona, quae lucebunt coram hominibus in laudem Dei cedent, omnibusque exemplo proderunt atque imitatione: ut ergo laus Dei celebrior fiat, simulque ut civibus suis exemplo prosit, optime facturum reor, si non clam officia haec virtutum praestiterit, sed palam. in quo illud observet, ne aliquis iure suspicari queat fieri ea palam propter ambitionem, aut aliquam improbam causam, sic enim dum exemplo prodesse vellet, multum obesset: id ergo si caverit, facturum optime arbitror, si palam, tum munificentia in aegenos, tum caeteris virtutum muneribus utatur. Nam inquit Christus, vos estis lux mundi. vicem igitur lucis praestare non pigeat.

Hoc vero nequaquam fiet, nisi virtutum officiis veluti luce quadam fulgentissima coram omnibus noster Episcopus luxerit. His officiis, quae ad impensas ac sumptus pertinere videntur, ea attinent, quae ad exigendos spectant reditus Episcopatus. Nam si hoc munus neglexerit, neque erga pauperes liberalitate ulla uti, neque divino cultui satisfacere poterit, providendum ergo pro viribus, ne reditus Episcopatus per inertiam pereant, se adhibeat diligentiam sedulusque curet, ne procurator urbanus, aut villicus bona pauperibus eroganda dilapidet, sed fidis ministris diligentissimisque utatur. qua in re illud cavendum est, ne a debitoribus, qui plerunque rustici sunt admodum aegeni, crudeliter ea quandoque villicus exigat, quae solvendo ipsi non sunt, nisi a filiis totaque familia victus extorquatur. Hoc nanque maxime alienum censeri debet a Christiana pietate, quodque in quovis

injunction of Augustine. For he says that the intention of the heart should remain hidden, but the good works yielded a profit if they are observed and shine forth like a light before men.[68] Let the bishop not seek from these duties praise for himself or any luster for his name (for that would be ambition) but God's praise. For this reason he will hold his intention secret, but the good works, which shine before men, will redound to God's praise and will profit everybody by example and imitation.[69] Therefore, in order that God's praise may be more celebrated and in order that at the same time his citizens may profit by his example, I judge that he will do best if he carries out these virtuous duties not secretly but openly. In this let him take care lest somebody rightly be able to suspect that these things are done openly out of ambition or some other wicked motive. For that way when he wants to help by good example he would be a great hinderance. If then he guards against that, I think he would do best if he openly exercises both generosity toward the needy and the other duties of the virtues. For as Christ says, "You are the light of the world."[70] Let him then not be ashamed to play the role of light.

But this will never happen unless our bishop shines forth before everybody by performing his virtuous duties like some brightly flashing light. To those duties which seem involved with expenses and expenditures are linked the things which look to raising the revenues of the bishopric. For if he neglects this task, he will not be able to make use of any generosity toward the poor or do justice to divine worship; therefore he must ensure as far as he can that the revenues of the bishopric do not waste away through laziness. Let him apply diligence and give intense care lest the city procurator or the country steward squander the goods earmarked for the poor; let him make use of trustworthy and energetic subordinates. On this point, he should take care lest the country steward sometimes make harsh demands from debtors, who are mostly rather needy peasants. They cannot pay these demands without snatching away the livelihood of their children and whole family. This should be judged utterly foreign to Christian piety, something which would be extremely rep-

---

[68] A computerized search of St. Augustine's works has failed to find this statement. Augustine does express similar sentiments in his sermon 54 and letter 140.

[69] Matt 5:15-16.

[70] Matt 5:14.

prophano sit valde reprehendendum, nedum in Episcopo Christiani gregis pastore, praeterea quaenam maior dementia esse potest, quam velle, dum inopum necessitati inservis, in egenos rusticos continuo crudelem esse, atque pietatis officium ab impietate auspicari? medium igitur tenorem quendam servabit: ne scilicet sinat per inertiam, aut cupiditatem ministrorum bona Episcopatus dilapidari, neve patiatur exactione pauperibus iniuriam fieri.

satis superque a nobis exposita videntur ea, quae ab Episcopo in seriis rebus praestanda sunt. Caeterum quoniam animus interdum requie indiget, quadamque curarum vacuitate: iccirco laxandus honestissimis iocis quandoque erit, alicuiusque secessus amoentate levaedus, ubi et deambulationibus et aucupiis, venationibusque et reliquis rusticis oblectationibus relaxari poterit. Hac enim ratione et animum recreabit, et valetudini consulet. Sed in iocis gravitatem servare oportet: neque sumptus faciendi in venationes et aucupia. Nihil enim magis Episcopo indecens magisque eius officio contrarium existimari debet, quam quae fiunt in huiusmodi res impensae. ab urbe vero non secedat, nisi iis diebus, quibus si secesserit, officio tamen non deerit.

Haec fere officia esse puto, quae pro operis nostri brevitate strictim collegenda censuimus. Reliqua [431] vero quae omissa sunt, ex horum similitudine facile intelligi posse existimo. Hactenus nobis disseruisse sufficiat de officio viri boni, ac probi Episcopi: quales nostra hac corruptissima tempestate pauci sunt. quamobrem nequaquam in animum inducas velim, aut turpe esse hisce temporibus aliorum vita ac moribus spretis, proprium quoddam sequi vivendi genus, aut difficile esse, ac prope impossibile muneribus hisce fungi, atque hanc vitae normam servare. Nam illud est in primis viri Christiani, nullo pacto duci humana laude, aut hominum iudicio, sed divina praecepta sibi servanda esse censere, quicquid de ipso loquantur homines, charumque et honorificum sibi putari si pro Christi nomine, ac Christiana vita dignus sit ignonimiam pati. de qua re Christi Apostolos plurimum gavisos sacrae literae testantur. deinde

rehensible in any layman, to say nothing of a bishop, the shepherd of the Christian flock. Besides, what greater madness can there be than to wish, while one is looking after the needs of the poor, to be simultaneously cruel to needy peasants and have the duty of piety performed under the aegis of impiety? He, therefore, will hold to a gentle mean: namely he will not allow the goods of the bishopric to be squandered through laziness or the rapacity of his subordinates, nor will he suffer exactions to inflict injury on poor people.

It seems that we have discoursed more than enough on the things which a bishop ought to do about serious concerns. But since the soul sometimes needs rest and some freedom from cares, sometimes he will need to relax with some gentlemanly jesting and to be uplifted by the beauty of some retreat where he will be able to relax by walking and bird watching and hunting and other rustic pleasures. This way he will both refresh his soul and take care for his health. But he should maintain his dignity in jesting, nor should expenses be incurred in hunting and bird watching. Let him regard nothing more unbecoming a bishop and nothing more contrary to his office than the expenses incurred on such things. He should not depart from the city except on those days on which he will not fall short of his duty if he leaves.

These are, I think, roughly the duties which we judged should be gathered and summarized, given the brevity of our work. I assume that the remaining things which were omitted can be easily understood from their similarity to these. May what has been discussed so far about the office of a good man and an upright bishop suffice us. Such men are very few in this corrupt time of ours. Therefore I would not want you to take to heart either that, spurning the life and morals of other people, it is shameful in these times to follow one's own way of life, or that it is difficult and almost impossible to perform these duties and preserve this standard of life. For it is a first requirement of a Christian man in no way to be led by human praise or men's judgment, but to be convinced that he must follow the divine commandments, regardless of what men say about him, and regard it as something dear and honorable for him if he is worthy to suffer ignominy for Christ's name and the Christian life. The sacred scriptures testify that Christ's apostles were extremely happy on this ac-

certo sciat frustra se hoc metu terreri: nam virtutis officia eo sunt praeclariora, quo maiora; neque vereri debet difficultatem ullam sibi fore in hac vivendi norma a nobis praescripta, si non in se, aut in virtute sua speraverit, sed tantum a Deo optimo auxilium imploraverit. Nullus enim qui eius ope confidit, vel in perquam arduis provinciis unquam defecit. Habes itaque Reverendissime praesul amici munus, neque re ipsa de qua tractat, neque te dignum, sed (ni fallor) ex animi nostri erga te propensione non ingratum omnino tibi futurum.

APPENDIX

Maiori arbitror diligentia maiorique nixu extirpanda est superstitio quam irreligiositas, quoniam hoc genere magis atque a pluribus peccatur quam impietate, adeo ut saepe numero mihi christiani videantur gentilium religionem [46r] imitari, in tantum a puritate divini cultus recessere. Nam fecimus nos quoque febris deum ac deum tabis, deam lippitudinis atque ophtalmiae. Rustici deos etiam bovum, ovium, segetumque invenere. Mitto mulieres apud quas nihil non superstitiosum. Quid dicam de tot figmentis miraculorum innumerisque aliis aucupiis lucri? Quid quod absque discrimine apocrypha scripta noveque inventa quaedam in eadem sunt authoritate fere a vulgo recepta qua scriptura canonica? Praetereo divinas quasdam preces quarum discretionem fecerunt ut aliae febri, aliae tabi, aliae capitis dolori medeantur. Enitendum episcopo est ut lenitate quadam omnes huiusmodi superstitiones obtruncet universumque populum revocet ad unius Dei ac Jesu Christi verum cultum. Nimirum doleo cum me huiusce rei memoria subit: paucos christianos reperias qui in adversa fortuna, aut mala [46v] valitudine recurrant ad deum ipsique preces fundant, quin potius plerisque omnes continuo precibus divos lacessunt prout a cuique libitum est, immo divorum simulacra. Quae omnia a christiana

count.[71] Besides, let him know for certain that this fear terrifies him to no purpose, for the duties of virtue are the more illustrious insofar as they are greater. Neither should he fear he will have any difficulty with this standard of life which we have enjoined if he shall have hoped not in himself or in his own strength but only if he shall have begged help from the good God. For nobody who trusts in his aid has ever failed, even in extremely difficult matters. So, reverend patron, you have the gift of a friend—not worthy of the subject it deals with nor of you, but (unless I am mistaken) it will not be completely unwelcome to you because of the good will of our heart toward you.

APPENDIX

I think that greater diligence and greater effort should be devoted to uprooting superstition than religious indifference because more people commit greater sins this way than by impiety, so much so that often times Christians seem to me to be imitating the religion of pagans, so far do they fall away from the purity of divine worship. For we make ourselves a god of fever and a god of pestilence, a goddess of glaucoma and of eye disease. The peasants also set up gods for cows, sheep, and grains. I pass over women, for whom nothing is without superstition! What shall I say about so many fake miracles and the countless other snares for money? What about the fact that the masses indiscriminately accept apocryphal writings[72] and certain newly discovered items with almost the same authority as the canonical scriptures? I skip certain divine prayers which they distinguish so that some may heal fever, some pestilence, some headaches. The bishop must strive so that by a certain gentleness he may cut away all this sort of superstitions and recall the whole people to the true worship of the one God and of Jesus Christ. It pains me when the memory of this business comes upon me; you will find few Christians who in hard luck or poor health seek recourse in God and pour out their prayers to God. Rather, they all immediately exasperate the saints, even the statues of the saints, with most of their prayers, just as each one pleases. All this is very foreign to Christian piety, which

---

[71] Acts 5:41.

[72] Here Contarini does not seem to have in mind what Protestants call the Apocrypha and Catholics call the deutero-canonical books, for two pages later he cites the book of Tobit along with other books of scripture.

pietate alienissima sunt quae praecipit Deum colendum esse in
spiritu et veritate ac in omnibus Deum amandum et omnia propter
Deum, ut nulla sit non tantum actio verum etiam nec cogitatio nostra
quae non tandem referatur in Deum, in quo est eminentissima unitas,
ad quam copulanda in unum sunt innumera hominum studia
multiplicesque cogitationes, ut et nos cum ipso unum, et invicem
unum simus. Non ergo, ut inquit apostolus Paulus, unicum divinum
cultum qui quantum fieri possit in unum colligendus est partimur in
plures. Non enim, ut inquit ipse, nos redemit aut Paulus, aut Apollo,
neque in nomine Pauli, aut Apollinis baptizati estis. Sed in nomine
[47r] Jesu Christi. Ad hunc igitur et omnes preces omnisque cultus
referantur.

Quo genere religiosi multum peccant: nam dum illi divi Francisci
religionem profitentur, hi vero beati Dominici, alii monachorum vitam vivunt, veluti divisus sit Christus, vicissim dissentiunt,
contenduntque ac inimicitias acerrimas exercent. Cuius rei illa
potissimum causa est quod non in unum illud sua studia contulere,
nec illius unius gloriam quaerunt. Hac enim ratione mirifice
convenirent neque aliqua in re studia eorum discreparent, sed eorum
cogitationes ab uno discendentes in plura divisae sunt ibique sistunt.
Hinc contentiones, rixae atque graves inimicitiae. Danda igitur sedulo
opera erit ut assuescant viri mulieresque qui christianam pietatem
profitentur colligere intentionem animi ad illud unum, in quo omnia venerentur, ne dum divos colunt obliviscantur summi Dei. Inquit
propheta ex persona domini, "Vacate et videte quoniam [47v] ego
sum Deus."

Neque formidandum est ne divi caeteri indignentur nobis ob
minutum eorum cultum divinumque auctum. Absit a christianis
mentibus sacrilegus hic timor. Nam si ob id eorum quos pro divis
colimus indignationem in nos irritari posse arbitraremur, continuo
fateri oporteret illos minime divos esse, sed malos quosdam demones

commands that God be worshipped in spirit and in truth and that God is to be loved in all things and that all things [are to be loved] because of God so that not only no action but not even any thought of ours should exist which is not finally referred to God, in whom is the highest unity to which all the countless pursuits and multiple thoughts of humans should be joined into one so that we are both one with him and one with one another. Therefore, as the Apostle Paul says, we do not divide up into many the unique divine worship which should be gathered together into one as far as possible. For as he himself says, "Paul or Apollo did not redeem us, nor were we baptized in the name of Paul or of Apollo. But in the name of Jesus Christ."[73] Therefore all prayers and all worship should be directed toward Him.

On this point the religious sin greatly, for while some profess the religious order of Saint Francis, others [profess that] of blessed Dominic; others live the life of monks, as if Christ has been divided up,[74] they disagree among themselves and squabble and engage in bitter hostilities. The main reason for this business is that they do not devote their energies to that one [object] nor do they seek the glory of him alone. On this point they agree marvelously together, nor do their endeavors differ on some point, but their thoughts flow down from one and are divided into many things and there they stand fast. From this [arise] squabbles, quarrels and deep hatreds. So there will be need to work hard so that men and women who profess Christian piety may gradually learn to direct their heart's intention toward that alone in whom they honor all things, lest they forget about the supreme God while worshipping the saints. The prophet says in the person of the Lord, "Stop and see that I am God."[75]

Neither should we fear lest those other saints become angry with us because their worship is curtailed and the divine [worship] increased. Far be this sacrilegious fear from Christian minds. If on this account we were to think that the wrath of those we worship as saints can be stirred up against us, we would immediately have to confess that they are not saints at all but some evil demons who corrupt divine worship. Augustine discusses this very clearly in his famous

---

[73] 1 Cor 1:12ff; 3:4ff.
[74] 1 Cor 1:13.
[75] Ps 46:11.

divinum cultum corrumpentes. Quod Augustinus in celebrrimo eo opere de civitate Dei luculentissime disserit. Sanctissimae namque illae angelorum mentes hominumque quae ad supremam foelicitatem divino munere sunt evectae idcirco foelices sunt, quia non amplius in se vivunt sed in Deum suum omnia earum studia collata. Eius laudem, eius honorem, eius denique gloriam quaerunt, suam negligunt quantoque sublimiorum sunt adeptae foelicitatis gradum, tanto magis haec earum menti sententia insidet. Immo haec fortasse potissima ratio [48r] est cur aliae sint aliis excellentiores. Legimus apud Thobiam de Raphaele angelo qui noluerit sibi a Thobia ullam laudem dari, sed Deo tantum cui et ipse serviret. Ex his considerare quilibet potest quam scelestum atque impium esset de supremis illis mentibus suspicari indignationem earum in nos concitari propterea posse quod divinum cultum auxerimus, earum cultu minuto opinione vulgi, sed re vera plurimum aucto. Nam hoc solo pacto potissimum suum cultum auctum censent si omnes summum bonum, scilicet Deum, coluerint, in quo ipsae praecipuae sunt et vivunt.

Omni ergo conatu huiusmodi generis superstitiones extirpandae sunt, atque harum inventores, quibus superstitio novum quoddam aucupium est, coercendi pro viribus ac poena mulctandi si ita opus esse quandoque visum fuerit. Horum multi in civitatibus reperiuntur, sed longe plures pagos, ac rura circumeunt ac ignaros rusticos [48v] multiplici fraude irretiunt. Hi et bovum divum et ovium ac vinearum segetumque invenere, adeo ut mihi saepius in memoriam revocent ea, quae Augustinus recitat ex Varrone excepta, de divis gentilium, qui innumeris rebus innumeram quoque deorum multitudinem adscrivere. Sicophantas hos episcopus noster diligenter perquirat, gravique mulcta afficat ne hisce monstris christiana puritas inquinetur. Superstitionis errore impietatisque scelere evitatis facile in recta religione populus poterit contineri.

work on the city of God.[76] For those most holy minds of angels and of men which by a divine gift have been carried up to supreme happiness are happy precisely because they no longer live for themselves, but with all their endeavors centered on their God, they seek his praise, his honor and finally his glory; they disregard their own [happiness], and the higher the level of happiness they have attained, the more this conviction dwells in their mind. Indeed, this may be the main reason why some are more excellent than others. We read in Tobit about the angel Raphael, who did not want Tobit to give any praise to him but to God alone, whose servant he too was.[77] From these things anybody can see how wicked and impious it would be to suspect those sublime minds of being able to be stirred to wrath against us because we increase divine worship, to the decrease of their worship in popular opinion but to its great increase in reality. For they regard their worship as enormously increased on this sole condition: if everybody worships the supreme good, namely God, in whom they above all exist and live.

Superstitions of this sort are to be uprooted by every effort, and their inventors, for whom a superstition is a new sort of snare, should be constrained with all your might and be subjected to punishment if sometimes this should seem needful. Many such men are found in the cities, but far more travel around the villages and countryside and ensnare ignorant peasants with their manifold trickery. They concoct the divinity of the cows and sheep and vineyards and grains, so much so that rather often they remind me of what Augustine relates, borrowing from Varro, about the divinities of the pagans, who attributed countless gods to countless objects.[78] Our bishop will carefully search out these tricksters and punish them severely lest Christian purity be defiled by these evil portents. When the error of superstition and the crime of impiety have been warded off, it will be easy to keep the people within the bounds of right religion.

---

[76] The reference is obscure; St. Augustine, *De civitate Dei*, II: 29, seems the best fit.

[77] Tob 12:17-20.

[78] Contarini seems to have in mind two passages from Saint Augustine's *De civitate Dei* (IV: 21 and 22 and VI: 9) which refer to Marcus Terentius Varro's (116-27 B.C.) lost *Antiquitatum rerum humanarum et divinarum libri XLI*, where Varro discussed the specific functions assigned to minor gods and goddesses.

INDEX

A

Aaron, 39
Ambrose, St., 12
Angelus, Joannes, 21
Apollo, 131
Apulia, 7
Aquinas; see Thomas Aquinas, St.
Augsburg Confession, 10
Augustine, St., 125, 131, 133
Aristotle, 14, 15, 22, 45, 73, 81,
    91, 109
Aristotelians; see Peripatetics
Averroists, 8

B

Barozzi, Pietro, 16, 85, 95, 121,
    123
Beccadelli, Ludovico, 18, 19
Belluno, 10, 19
Bergamo, 14, 27
Bibliography, 23, 24
Bibliotheca Vaticana, 21
Bologna, 11, 18, 27
Borromeo, Carlo; see Carlo Borromeo,
    St.
Borromeo, Federico, 13
Botero, Giovanni, 12
Brescia, 9
Bucer, Martin, 11

C

Caesar, Julius, 95
Carafa, Gianpietro; see Paul IV
Castiglione, Baldassar, 12
Cavanzzana Romanelli, Francesca, 23
Censorship, 18-21
Cervia, 9
Charles V, 9, 10, 11
Clement VII, 9
Clodius, 95
Colonna, Vittoria, 10
Contarini, Alvise [Gasparo's father], 7
Contarini, Alvise [Gasparo's nephew],
    8, 18, 19

Contarini family, 7, 17
Contarini, Gasparo:
    churchman, 10, 11
    education, 7, 8
    magistrate, 9, 10
    scholar, 8
    writer:
        Confutatio articulorim seu
            questionum Lutheranorum,
            10
        De immortalitate animae, 8,
            17
        De magistratibus et Republica
            Venetorum, 8, 9, 10, 18
        De officio viri boni et probi
            episcopi, 12-22;
            see also *Office of a Bishop*
        De potestate pontificis quod
            divinitus sit tradita 10
        Defense of the Regensburg
            Formula on Justification, 11
        Opera, 18-20
        Primae philosophiae com-
            pendium, 10
Contarini, Giulio, [Gasparo's nephew,
    Bishop of Belluno], 19
Cortese, Paolo, 12
Council of Ten, 9

D

Dandolo, Matteo, 19
David, 29, 71
Della Casa, Giovanni, 12, 19
Diet of Worms, 9
Dionysius the Areopagite, 61
Dittrich, Franz, 23
Dominic, St., 131

E

Eck, Johann, 11
Egypt, 7

F

Florence, 8, 19

Foscarari, Egidio, 19
Fragnito, Gigliola, 17, 21, 23
Francis, St., 131
Francis I, 9

G

Geneva, 11
Giberti, Gian Matteo, 13
Gilbert, Felix, 23
Giustiniani, Lorenzo, 12
Giustiniani, Tommaso, 8
Gleason, Elisabeth, 23, 24
Gregory the Great, St., 12
Gropper, Johannes, 11

H

Hercules, 41
Hincmar, Bishop of Rheims, 12
Horace [Flaccus], 43, 101

I

Ignatius of Loyola, St., 12
Inquisition, 18, 20

J

Jay, Claude, 12
Jedin, Hubert, 13
Jesuits, 10
John Chrysostom, St. 12

K

Kristeller, Paul Oskar, 22

L

Lippomano, Nicolao, 14
Lippomano, Pietro, 13, 14, 16, 21,
    22, 27
Logan, Oliver, 23
Luther, Martin, 8, 9, 10

M

Machiavelli, Niccolò, 12
Manuzio, Aldo, 20
Manuzio, Paolo, 19
Matheson, Peter, 24

Medici, Marco, 20
Melanchthon, Phililpp. 11
Minnich, Nelson, 24
Modena, 18, 19
Morone, Giovanni, 10, 11, 18, 19
Moses, 39, 71

O

Ochino, Bernadino, 11, 18
Office of a bishop–other books on the
    subject, 12, 13
The Office of a Bishop:
    Circumstances of its composition,
        13, 14, 29-31
    Circumstances of its printing,
        17-20
    Contents:
        Absenteeism, 69
        Advising his people, 87
        Angels, 33
        Charity, 63-71
        Christology, 59
        Concupiscible part of the
            soul, 37-43
        Divine office, 79-85, 93
        Dignity of a bishop, 35
        Dining, 89
        Eucharist, 77, 109
        Faith, 59, 61, 63
        Fortitude, 47
        Gentleness, 53
        God's image in creatures, 31,
            37
        Governing his servants, 95
        Heresy, 107
        Hope, 63
        Hospitals, 123
        Irascible part of the soul, 37,
            39, 47, 53
        Justice, 53, 55
        Liberality, 45
        Magic, 105
        Magnanimity, 49, 51
        Magnificence, 51
        Mass, 85
        Music, 89
        Natural inclination to God,
            73, 75
        Nuns, 113

Orders, Holy, 77
Parsimony, 121
Penance, sacrament of, 77, 109
Perfection, 31
Poets who encourage lust,
    45, 101
Poor, care for the, 119-129
Pope, 77, 103
Preaching, 105
Priesthood, 77
Prudence, 55
Punishing bad clergy, 99, 103
Recreation, 91, 93
Religious orders, 31, 97, 103,
    131
Sacraments, 75
Saints, cult of, 131
Sick, care for the, 95, 97
Sleep, 93
Superstitions, 109, 129, 133
Temperance, 43
Vacationing in countryside, 93
Vicars, 89
Wealth, proper use of, 119, 121
Women, care for, 105, 115,
    117, 129
Women's clothing and
    ornaments, 115, 117
Manuscript differences from the
    printed text, 21, 22, 128-33
Structure of the treatise, 14, 16
Variations in the three printed
    editions, 20, 21
Olin, John, 24

P

Padua, 16, 85, 123
Padua, University of, 7, 8, 9, 10
Paleotti, Gabriele, 13
Paris, University of, 20
Paul, St., 71, 103, 115, 117, 131
Paul III, 10
Paul IV, 11, 18, 19, 21
Peripatetics, 8, 10, 53, 55
Pflug, Julius, 11
Piton, M., 13, 24
Pius IV, 18
Plato, 35, 91, 109
Pole, Reginald, 10, 18
Pomponazzi, Pietro, 7, 8

Praxiteles, 63

Q

Querini, Vincenzo, 8

R

Raphael, 131
Ravenna, 9
Rebiba, Scipione, 20
Regensburg, Colloquy of, 11
Rome, 9, 18, 19
Ross, James Bruce, 24
Rückert, Hanns, 24

S

Savonarola, Girolamo, 17
Solomon, 41, 43
Spain, 9, 10
Spirituali, 10, 19

T

Tellechea Idigoras, José, 13, 24
Thomas Aquinas, St., 14, 15, 22
Tobit 133
Tramontin, Silvio, 24
Trent, Council of, 19
Truchsess, Cardinal, 12

V

Valerio, Agostino, 13
Varro, 133
Veneto, 7
Venice, 7, 9, 10, 18
Vermigli, Peter Martyr, 11, 18
Vettori, Pietro, 19
Virgil, 65, 111

Z

Zenario, Damiano, 20